March 8, 1989   .95

Dearest,
IN EVERY KIND OF LIGHT!
Love
Tyan

IN A
Different
Light

An anthology
of
lesbian writers

Edited by
Carolyn Weathers
and Jenny Wrenn

CLOTHESPIN FEVER PRESS

LOS ANGELES □ 1989

Cover art: Judye A. Best
Book design: Jenny Wrenn

Copyright © 1989 each author

Copyright © 1989 this collection, Clothespin Fever Press

Cataloging information

Weathers, Carolyn

In a different light: an anthology of lesbian writers.

1. American literature —Women authors.
2. Lesbian's writings, American—Fiction 3. Lesbianism—Poetry
4. Lesbianism—Fiction
I. Wrenn, Jenny   II. Title
PS508.W7   813.0922   88-92419
ISBN: 0-9616572-5-1

"Best of L.A.," from the *L. A. Weekly* :1978 Best of L.A. issue, ©1987.   Reprinted by permission of the *L.A. Weekly.*

S. Diane Bogus, "The Creator's Dalliance #4, " "Lady Godiva," "Mayree," from *Sapphire's Sampler,* WIM publications, copyright© 1982 by S. Diane Bogus. Reprinted by permission of the author.
    "Small Time Profundity #2," from *Woman in the Moon*, WIM Publications, copyright © 1977 by S. Diane Bogus. Reprinted by permission of the author.

Jeri Castronova, "The Magic Feather," from *Shadow of the Goddess*, Celebration Press, copyright ©1984 by Jeri Castronova. Reprinted by permission of the author.

Judy Grahn, "1960, Skeletons in Sergeant's Kirk's Closet," from *Another Mother Tongue*, copyright ©1984 by Judy Grahn. Reprinted by permission of Beacon Press.

Eloise Klein Healy, "A Mile Out Of Town," from *A Packet Beating Like a Heart*," Books Of A Feather Press, copyright © 1980 by Eloise Klein Healy. Reprinted by permission of the author.
    "To Speak for Human Feelings," from *Ordinary Wisdom*, Paradise Press, copyright© 1980 by Eloise Klein Healy. Reprinted by permission of the author.

ACKNOWLEDGEMENTS

We would like to thank the following:

Ann Bradley for having the vision to establish the *Lesbian Writers Series* and the sense of purpose to keep it going and growing.

Ayofemi Stowe Folayan who stepped in and helped with her superb proofreading and editorial assistance during the last two months of preparation when we were faced with the illness and death of one of our beloved mothers, Alida Weathers Hayen, of Fort Worth, Texas.

Carmen Silva for proofreading the works in Spanish and for translating "Encarrajuda" into English.

Sharon Lilly and Joan Potter for their undying faith in us; for cheerfully reading through an early manuscript--a proto anthology--and sharing their comments; for their unwavering encouragement.

Gail Suber for proofreading the final manuscript.

Kim Zamarin and *Camille Loya* for reading and commenting on the manuscript.

Kate O'Brien , as always, for her everlasting love and faith in us.

Margy Tuck for her ongoing moral support.

Richard Labonte and the staff of A Different Light Books for good will and unfailing helpfulness.

Bookstores everywhere--from **A Different Light** in Los Angeles, **Page One** in Pasadena, **Sisterhood** in West L.A., **A Different Drummer** in Newport Beach, to all those across the country, in every state, to those outside the United States and around the world--that provide readings by lesbian writers and help keep our lively arts flourishing.

Carolyn Weathers and Jenny Wrenn, Editors
Los Angeles, California
November 25, 1988

TABLE OF CONTENTS

Preface: Through the Glass Brightly

WRITING THE PREFACE for this anthology creates a prism effect; a myriad of reflected hues are contained in the memories of these last five years. I am proud of the results and of the endurance and fortitude that were necessary to create and nurture what has become one of the finest consistent writers series in this country: the *Lesbian Writers Series*. I am also exhilarated with this book and by the artistry, vision and delicate strength which were combined to create it.

The source of the light began on a rainy January night in 1984, when I made a three-hour, rush-hour trip with Carolyn Weathers to Newport Beach to hear her read at Three Guineas Bookstore. There are some memories that move us through the rest of our lives--that evening is one of them.

The rain had eliminated all but five intrepid souls from the cozy sanctuary of Pam Roberts' now sadly closed bookstore. For the forty or so minutes that it took for Carolyn to complete her translucent memoir of her childhood, *Leaving Texas*, her audience floated in the lovely territory attained when the sense, heart and soul blend. The artist and her audience achieved a radiant symbiosis.

This experience encouraged me to act on a dream that I'd had for a number of years, to found a writer's series specifically to showcase and celebrate the talents of lesbians. Once the dream is out of the proverbial golden box, the work takes over.

In its early stages, the *Lesbian Writers Series* and I were indebted to some entirely noble and generous souls (men included!), who attended every single month and brought their friends. My efforts were supported by my admirable colleagues at **A Different Light Books,** Richard Labonte, John Ruggles and, later on, by Ron Whiteaker and Jim Morrow.

I am also grateful to Eloise Klein Healy, Katherine Forrest and Terry Wolverton, who regularly sent prospective writers as well as listeners.

I have been asked, over the years, what inspired me to begin the *Series*. First was hearing Carolyn Weathers read her work that magical, rainy night in Newport Beach and knowing I wanted her to inaugurate the *Series*. Second, I had regularly attended readings throughout California and had been keenly aware that, while these events included numerous lesbians, this aspect of the writer's identity was never acknowledged. In some cases it was the writer herself who never discussed, either in her work or in her introduction, that she was a lesbian. This disturbed me, and I wanted to do something about it.

It was never my purpose, however, in establishing the *Series* to manipulate any commonality, for certainly we are as diverse as the shafts of light from our rainbow. But I was too uncomfortable by the constraint and silence regarding who we were to walk away from it.

In establishing the *Series,* it was my intent and goal to radiantly acknowledge and formally celebrate the literary achievements, artistry and brilliance of a highly diverse community of women. The *Series* was created to make that acknowledgement with pride, bravado and quality. It was indeed my primary goal to create and develop one of the finest writer's series in the nation, not simply a gathering for lesbians-only or one lacking depth and skill in the participants. I am indeed proud that as the *Series* ends its fifth year, the caliber of the participants is extraordinary.

The anthology that you now hold contains a proud history of achievement by lesbians, women who put pen to paper, paper to press and press to people. Initially, let us thank the lesbian publishers of the past and those alive today, including Clothespin Fever Press and its magnificent artistic collaboration of Carolyn Weathers and Jenny Wrenn. Their union is providing us with a rich harvest.

I would be remiss if I did not thank KPFK's "IMRU," the

gay/lesbian radio program for interviewing me in the second year of the program and allowing wider promotion of the *Series*.

Let me also thank my sisters and colleagues in other bookstores, gay/lesbian and feminist, such as **Page One** in Pasadena and **Sisterhood** in Westwood, who provide the space for writers to read and distribute their work.

I am delighted that many writers have made their first public appearance on the *Series*. I am thoroughly pleased that nationally acknowledged writers have come to see the *Lesbian Writers Series* as an important gig.

As was stated in the "Best of L.A." issue of the *L.A. Weekly* in 1987:

*As girls, we scoured our health textbook and Webster's Third for any small mention of the "L word." In college, we voraciously devoured **The Well of Loneliness**, Mary McCarthy's **The Group** and Sappho's fragmented poetry, still hunting for some mention of the Love That Dare Not Speak Its Name. Well, that Love—being no longer bound nor gagged (as tightly, anyway)— has found its voice. There's been a veritable explosion in available lesbian fiction and non-fiction in the past few years. Continuing a tradition that began in 1984, A Different Light Bookstore in Silver Lake presents a Lesbian Writers Series, where women who identify as lesbians can read their poetry and prose; unpublished talent, as well as big names have been featured. Curated by former bookstore employee Ann Bradley, this event takes place monthly (how appropriate!).*

Finally, I thank the audience and the readers. You are the crystals which catch the light. Without you, we'd all be in darkness. Blessings.

Ann Bradley
Los Angeles, California
December 1988

Introduction: On Anthologies and the Lesbian Literary Tradition

THE EXPERIENCE IS FAMILIAR--wondering if so and so writer is a lesbian--wondering if so and so artist at the gallery is, or which actress in the play. By all the laws of averages, some of them are--but, since no one is saying--which ones? In that anthology of women writers chosen from the shelf at the library--which ones are lesbians? It is not that our satisfaction is predicated only on finding our crowd. Or that those who are lesbians must always write about something "issue related"--the eclectic subjects do appeal. But we want lesbian writers to be identified for who they are. The invisibility of lesbian achievement that stratifies cultural accomplishments leaves a lingering "outsider" feeling that belies our presence.

This anthology is based upon writers who read at *The Lesbian Writers Series* of Los Angeles' A Different Light Bookstore between 1984 and 1988. The *Series* was organized in 1984 by Ann Bradley, who still curates it, and it is still going strong. The *Series* has given voice to the multifaceted lesbian community, a community comprised of women, and as such emphasizes the family and financial concerns specific to women. This culture survives within a heterosexual one that designates its poets, short story writers, and novelists as men. W.H. Auden, Edgar Allen Poe, John Steinbeck, are the standards of college courses. Women are scarce when one examines the leaders in literature, Emily Dickinson, Katherine Mansfield, and Jane Austen. The lesbians are even fewer because of their invisibility: Emily Dickenson, perhaps, certainly Gertrude Stein, Sara Orne Jewett, Willa Cather, and Carson McCullers (many, many others, of course). Several great women writers are just beginning to appear in the litera-

ture anthologies used in universities. Interestingly, the first
Book of the Month selection, *Lolly Willowes,* a very well-
received book in 1926, was by Sylvia Townsend Warner, a
lesbian. The work, forgotten by the dominate culture today,
has been reissued and is known to those who keep this hidden
culture alive.

Instead of maintaining our culture through public librar-
ies, civic arenas or galleries, lesbians have frequently grav-
itated toward private centers, initially bar rooms, small community centers, and private homes, finally bookstores. Our
growth and development as a culture has progressed mainly
through the underground for fear of ridicule and dismissal.

We've often been described within the context of the pre-
vailing heterosexual limelight--as if we were a reaction
against that society. To those unfamiliar with the lesbian
community our only distinguishing difference is that we refuse to sleep with men. In *A Plain Brown Rapper* by Rita Mae
Brown (1976), she writes, "The male party line concerning
Lesbians is that women become Lesbians out of reaction to
men." "This," she admonishes, "is a pathetic illustration of
the male ego's inflated proportions." She goes on to point out
that lesbians seek the company of other women because they
enjoy their company.

A look into one public library's card catalog shows the
limited view of lesbians to which Rita Mae Brown was refer-
ring. For the book, *The Lesbian in America,* the catalog card
summary reads, "Characteristics, problems, social organiza-
tion and legal status of female sex deviates in the United
States." Another card in the same public library's catalog for
the book, *Woman Plus Woman,* reads, "A refutation of so-
called myths and misconceptions, discussing lives of historic
figures and writings both scientific and literary." For those
who view the heterosexual community as the only community possible, lesbianism remains a sexual deviation and a

sickness.

Those who work to put together lesbian anthologies face the task of implicitly or explicitly presenting who the lesbian is and what her way of life is. A woman's press in London, Onlywomen Press, published an anthology of lesbian poets in 1986 titled *Beautiful Barbarians: lesbian feminist poetry*. In the foreword the editors write, "We write without the context of a well established or widely known lesbian literary tradition or an acknowledged way of life. So, recent lesbian anthologies have tried to be inclusive, even representative."

To acknowledge a lesbian culture has too often been met with disdain, distrust, and disbelief as the quoted library catalog cards have manifested when they repeatedly used the words "so-called" for conceptions about lesbians being anything but sexual deviants.

The plethora of books devoted to the theme of "coming out"--one person's own revelation of herself as a lesbian to her parents, friends and co-workers--demonstrates the fear of ridicule, distrust, hatred and ostracism many of us have to overcome before we can believe in ourselves and know that our lives are unique, different, and incredibly rich and wonderful.

Many lesbians have, fortunately, moved past the stereotypes and misconceptions that have threatened to stifle the making of a lesbian culture, and the resulting literary tradition is growing and flourishing. The burgeoning of gay/lesbian and feminist bookstores, a development of recent decades, has not only provided the resource centers for lesbian works. Through the sponsoring of authors' readings in their stores, such as *The Lesbian Writers Series*, they have further enriched our own validation, the belief in our literary prowess.

Anthologies by their very nature reflect not only the authors themselves but the variation of form and content. An editor of an anthology of established short story writers, both American and European, writes, "Here are stories long and short; serious and grave stories are mixed with light and humorous ones; and next to rugged tales of love are tales of the bizarre and the unusual." Their commonality is the vehicle of expression, literary form, and our commonality is such as well.

The lesbian writers presented here work in a number of different forms: poetry, short story and the novel. Within the traditional structure are the variations and adaptations many of the writers have made to extend the medium. Ruchele ZeOeh, in particular, creates sounds with words and their juxtapositions. The reader moves through her poems as if dancing or skipping along the paths her words make. Another poet, M'Lissa Mayo, takes the reader into an art world that challenges traditional concepts of meaning and truth. The impression is reminiscent of Futurism and the Dada movement. Jeri Castronova, on the other hand, harks back to an earlier form of poetry with an almost periodic sentence approach to capture a magical world partly past and partly futuristic. Word order is occasionally reversed to enhance the other-worldly atmosphere necessary to her themes.

Another writer deeply concerned with atmosphere is Chaney Holland, whose novella excerpt plays with an inner and external landscape through a first person narration. Atmosphere is also important to the novel excerpt of Lynette Prucha but in a different way. Her use of atmosphere, sophistication and dry wit works to fashion a highly stylistic satire of the detective thriller.

Many of the other writers have worked more with the themes and the content of their stories than with form itself. Here the range extends from the political, the tragic, the humorous, the bizarre to the erotic. Gloria Ramos' story takes the reader for a subway ride that surprises as well as unnerves in a classic almost Aristotelean completeness. Jess Wells tells a story with a straight forwardness that leads the reader into a bizarre tragedy that comments on the complexity of everyday existence. In a prose/poem Eileen Pagan uses everyday Puerto Rican speech, a unique and colorful dialect, to transport the reader to her childhood and to her later immigration.

The anthology begins with a fantasy by Nancy Tyler Glenn that in itself reflects the diversity that the works to follow exhibit. All of the works presented were selected for their literary quality as well as the range of themes and styles. Rather than group the works by medium, poetry in one section, short stories in another and so on, the works were carefully placed to create a flow, one to another. The effect of the whole has created a symphony to allow the reader to begin at the beginning and read through to the end. Anthologies can sometimes be difficult to read because of the changes in style, content and theme. For this reason many anthologies have sought to overcome the problems of diversity by grouping works thematically, or chronologically, or as mentioned by form. While such categorization has given a very readable structure to many anthologies, we chose a more orchestrated approach that mixes the different players for a cohesive symphony that celebrates how diversity creates the whole. We felt it fitting that we actually ended the anthology with a song by Pauline Moore.

Jenny Wrenn
Los Angeles, California
November 25, 1988

Nancy Tyler Glenn

THE BOOK PEOPLE

"Is ANYONE OUT THERE?" Kay tried to keep her voice low. She didn't want to awaken the sleeping slob slouched in the chair in front of the typewriter. Using both hands she braced against the platen trying to push herself up. "This is what I get for working for a man," she grumbled. "If I ever get out of this machine, I'll never—"

"Are you trapped? I didn't realize he was still writing your scene when he fell asleep."

Kay turned her head. Her co-worker, Joy, was perched on an empty typewriter ribbon spool on the cluttered desk. "Not so loud!" she whispered. "Do you want to wake jerko?"

Joy laughed. "Nothing could stir that myth-monkey." She eased herself off the spool and walked over to the old-fashioned typing machine. "I think I can get you out of here. Take a deep breath." She climbed onto the typewriter and pushed the carriage return key with her foot until Kay was free.

Kay grabbed the bail and worked her way along the platen until she could grasp the paper guide. One good upward push and she was out. She slid down the casing, barely missing the TAB key.

Joy had walked around the typewriter to meet her. "Do you need any help?"

"I think I can make it the rest of the way." Kay grabbed the top of the wire basket holding the manuscript and climbed down easily. When she reached the top of the desk she took off her high heeled shoes and flung them as far as she could.

Joy looked alarmed. "He's going to be pissed as hell when he wakes up and finds you barefoot."

Kay rubbed her feet. "He's going to be pissed as hell when he wakes up and find me *gone!*"

"You're leaving before he finishes the story?" Joy was fascinated.

"Yes, dammit and I think you should too."

"I've thought of quitting but never before a job was completed. How will that look on your resume?"

Kay shrugged. "It's happened to every writer. They expect it from time to time. I try not to make it a habit, but I'm going to enjoy thwarting this sleaze. How long have you worked for him?"

Joy thought for a minute. "About three years. It was a career change for me. I started out in dreams, but people rarely remembered them and frankly, in the last few years dreams have become terrifying with all the nasty things happening on the planet. This is easy by comparison."

"I know," Kay agreed. "But why work for this guy? There are plenty of good writers. Don't you get the trades?"

Joy looked abashed. "I do and I would really love to work for some of the women writers advertising for characters, but I don't interview very well and this is a steady job."

Kay shook her head. "It isn't worth it. You're a talented character and could get work anywhere. I've worked for some wonderful women in all parts of the world. They've always put me in very interesting settings and given me delightful co-characters. These days I can get as much work as I want."

Joy stepped back. "I recognize you now. I didn't at first because of the way he dressed you."

"And undressed me." Kay scowled. "I hadn't worked for a man for so long I forgot what is was like."

"I loved you in that Sci-fi novel, but I thought you should have had the lead," Joy said.

"I tried out for it but I look terrible in black and white. I need brighter colors. Besides I was too old for the part. I think it was cast excellently."

"I really admire your work," Joy murmured. "I noticed that for the past few years you've only worked for...."

"Lesbians." Kay nodded. "For the past five years I've worked exclusively for lesbians."

Joy sighed. "That must be heaven. Are you a...a—"

"Yes." Kay said.

"Then why would you want to work here?" Joy asked.

"I was between jobs. I'm signed up for a great part later this year."

Joy looked puzzled. "But you don't need the work. Why didn't you just take a vacation?"

Kay looked at her. "There's another reason."

"What is it?"

Kay smiled. "I wanted to meet you. I'd heard glowing reports about you and after seeing your work I was fascinated."

Joy's heart pounded. "Thank you."

Kay took her hand and squeezed it. "Every woman I've met who's worked with you says the same thing: 'Get her out of that place. She's got too much talent to stay in a dead end job.'"

"I wish I could believe it."

"Believe it," Kay urged. "Come with me and let me prove it to you. If you aren't convinced, I'll come back with you and finish this job."

Joy took a deep breath. "It's a deal."

"Would you like to drive or just be there?"

"It's been a long time since I've been on the road, but under the circumstances I'd prefer to just be there."

"Hang on."

"This is my retreat," Kay said a little proudly. "It's where I come between jobs."

Joy was dazzled. "Wasn't this the site for one of the novels you starred in a couple of years ago?"

"No, but it's an exact duplicate. I loved it so much I had it built by a building contractor friend of mine from Half Moon Bay. She did a terrific job. It's all wood, pebble and glass. You won't find a single molecule of plastic in the whole place."

Joy's eyes moved slowly around the living room taking in the careful details. "It's exquisite, and there's such a feeling here of being totally safe."

"It is safe here," Kay assured her. "Nothing but wilderness and quiet for miles and miles and miles."

"Aren't you afraid of the wild animals?"

"No," Kay said quietly. "And they aren't afraid of me."

Neither of them felt the need to speak for a long time and then they looked at each other and laughed.

"We *are* a couple of characters," Joy said. "You're standing there in a slinky dress in your stocking feet and I'm dressed in these stupid tight pants and spiked heels. We're both wearing enough makeup to cause our faces to fall."

"I'll be right back," Kay promised.

After Kay left the room Joy went over to the bookcase. There were shelves and shelves of lesbian titles. She had read many of them. Others she had promised herself she would read, but had never gotten around to it. She always said she was too busy but the truth was, they made her sad. Working in that dingy office for the last three years, never having the courage to quit and audition for some of these roles. She felt ashamed.

Kay came back into the room. She had changed into a soft bathrobe and had another robe on her arm for Joy.

"I didn't realize there were so many lesbian books," Joy said.

Kay laughed. "Check out my library. These are just the

ones I played in. It's sort of a trophy case."

"I didn't know you had starred in so many."

"Oh, I didn't star in all of them. I like bit parts too and," she plucked a book off the shelf and handed it to Joy, "in a few of them I just played stand-in."

Joy turned the book over in her hand. She had read it. "I don't remember seeing you in it."

"Look closer. I played all the love scenes. The protagonist was very young and felt too shy to play them. I get a lot of work that way. I like doing it. It's easy work and it makes me feel, well...like a teacher. I think of it as educational."

"I've certainly learned a few things from books," Joy admitted.

Kay handed her the robe. "Down the hall and to the left."

"I read the book," Joy said slyly. "I remember where the bathroom is."

"You'll find everything you need. Help yourself to anything in the closet. I kept most of my costumes."

Joy eased herself into the bath. She felt the warm soothing water wash away all the grime from her former job. She knew she wouldn't be going back. She couldn't go back. It didn't bother her that she was walking out before the book was finished. It wasn't an important book. In fact, she admitted to herself, it was trash. She was amazed that any of her real talent had come through.

She looked through Kay's closet and selected a pair of slacks and sweater from a book she had really wanted to audition for.

Kay was sitting in front of the fireplace. She turned when Joy came back into the room. "Yes, you would have been perfect in that part. I'm sure the author would agree."

Joy was pleased. "Thank you. I think you did a terrific job, but I agree with you."

"Have a seat." Kay moved to make room on the sofa. "I was just looking through the trades. You aren't going to have a bit of trouble finding suitable work."

"I think you should know, I'm not going back to that place. I'd rather go back to dreams than spend another dreary minute in that grimy hack factory."

"You aren't going to have to go back to dreams. There are so many challenging roles for you to play. You'll have trouble choosing. There are that many. You look through this while I clean up and then we'll have something to eat and talk about it. I can probably give you some tips about the authors." Kay handed her the magazine and got up. "I can't wait to get rid of this makeup."

Joy flipped through the pages of Lesbian Characters Guild. She was amazed at the number of jobs and character descriptions.

COMIC BOOK CHARACTERS NEEDED. Must be action oriented. Characters should be able to enunciate words like, "Pow!" and "Arggh!" while leaping through the air.

NEEDED: PROTAGONISTS FOR LESBIAN WEST-ERN ADVENTURE. Bring own outfit and horse. Please, no English saddles.

FUTURIST WRITER LOOKING FOR CHARACTERS. Characters must have ability to imagine a world at peace in which the superior intellectual abilities of women are acknowledged by all.

LESBIAN CHARACTERS OF ALL NATIONALITIES AND RACES NEEDED. Author is desperate. Please apply in person.

YOUNG WRITER NEEDS WHIMSICAL CHARAC-TERS FOR FIRST NOVEL. Experience preferred.

NIGHT WORKERS. Writer only able to work evenings and weekends. All characters must have flexible schedules.

LESBIAN REGENCY WRITER NEEDS CHARAC-

TERS. Production will be in full costume. Knowledge of English history is helpful, as well as fads and mannerisms of the day.

POWER CHARACTERS NEEDED BY ECO-FEMINISTS. Smokers need not apply.

FEMS AND BUTCHES NEEDED FOR FIRST PERSON ROMANCE STORIES. Mid-Western writer looking for characters for true-to-life light reads of no more than 5000 words.

S/M WRITER LOOKING FOR CHARACTERS FOR LOVING STORY. Bring your own gear.

HEARING IMPAIRED CHARACTERS NEEDED BY VISION IMPAIRED WRITER FOR UNIQUE DETECTIVE NOVEL. Some knowledge of Braille and computers would be helpful.

Kay came back into the room toweling her hair. "Find anything interesting?"

Joy was incredulous. "I found everything interesting. I'm tempted by the Western but the one that really sounds fantastic is the Futurist writer.

Kay's face became animated. "I was hoping it would intrigue you. I have a part in it myself and have already told the author about you. She seemed interested."

"Really?" Joy couldn't conceal her excitement. "Are you starring in it?"

"No, there is no star system in this novel. I have a good part. I play the mother of one of the characters."

"Aren't you a little young?" Joy asked.

"Not for this novel. In the future, without the stress of war and disease, the characters don't age as fast."

After dinner the two sat in front of the fireplace and talked about the most exciting job in the world. Being characters in lesbian novels and stories was more exciting than any job they could think of, except maybe writing lesbian novels and stories.

Finally Kay turned to Joy. "It's getting late and tomorrow is a busy day. I can make up the bed in the guest room or you can come in and stretch out with me."

Joy was quiet for a while. Finally she said, "I...I...I find you very attractive but I'm still processing my feelings from my last relationship. I don't know that I'm ready to have sex with anyone yet."

Kay reached over and brushed Joy's arm with her fingertips. "I wasn't suggesting sex. I find you attractive too, in many ways. In stories and novels I quite often have sex. It's a job and I do it well. In my own life I like to be more organic. If I stretch out with you, it's to be with you. If nothing happens, then nothing happens. If something does happen...."

Joy grinned happily. "Then, that's *another* story."

Lynette Prucha

Smokescreen

a novel excerpt

Smokescreen is a novel about the mystery of love and counterfeit passions. The city's Los Angeles and the heroine is Mercedes Martini, an ingenue private eye, a Sam Spade in drag. Unwittingly, Martini is immersed in a complicated intrigue that begins with the theft of an antique dance-card, leads to the disappearance of her best friend, Mona Lisa, and lures Martini into encounters with various adversaries, the most lethal being the stunning, villainous, Rachel Mann. The following episode begins at Derringer's, the most popular lesbian bar in Los Angeles. Mercedes doesn't know that Mona Lisa stole the antique, only that Mona Lisa called the night before to say she was in some kind of trouble. She tells Mercedes to expect a package (which turns out to be the stolen antique dance-card) and sets a meeting time that following evening at Derringer's. Now, Martini has the antique, and everyone wants it, including Rachel Mann.

Derringer's

REGAN SURVEYED THE WOMEN waiting to get into Derringer's. It promised to be a busy night. In a town that opened and closed lesbian bars like venetian blinds, Derringer's hadn't yet hit the mortality list. As clubs for women go, it was tidy; the drinks were cheap; the women, well, they weren't cheap, but a damn lot of them were easy to be had. Just ask Regan.

At twenty-seven, Regan had cultivated a saloon philosophy suited for this stone-hearted town. She never mixed business with anyone's pleasure; she was careful to separate the Dos Equis of this world from the Dom Perignons; she never touched a mixed drink and made it a point to keep her nose clean during working hours. She kept her back to the door, never letting anyone push her up against a wall; the only tips she took came from the top, and once she stepped on someone's toes, she never looked back.

Regan made her way inside the club, surreptitiously eyeing the curves on line, same faces, some prettier than others, and tried to locate her target for the night. But Torch, a pink champagne-blonde checker, derailed Regan and motioned for her help. Regan pushed her way back through the line to Torch. "What's up?" she asked, impatient.

"I'll tell you what's up. It ain't me," the gum-chewing rock n' roller said. "I'm suffering from a serious case of claustrophobia. These broads like to hang around and argue about the cover." She blew a bazooka bubble in Regan's face. "It's not my fault they can't remember the damn thing."

"So what's the problem?" Regan said to a tall, tough-looking brunette with spiked bands on her wrists and a leather jacket tied around her slim waist. "Either you got the card or you ain't got the card. This isn't supposed to be hard."

"I told her I got my I.D., but I left my membership card home," the girl said, with a sour expression curdling her face.

"So tonight you pay eight bucks and next time we get you in for five."

The brunette was pissed. She threw her hands up in the air, turning to the girls in line behind her to complain.

Regan didn't have time for bullshit. She didn't want to lose Mercedes in the crowd. "There's no issue here. If you don't pay, you don't get in. Simple   I got a lot of thirsty women on line who are gonna trample us flat if you don't cough up the bucks," Regan said, taking charge.

The girl threw a wad of crumbled bills on the register. Torch took her sweet time counting them. "Like they say on TV, don't leave home without it." Then she smiled a big one. The brunette looked like she was going to deck Torch, but Regan gently pushed her through the door, politely showing her the way.

"Hey, we ain't got all night," yelled Lynn, a pert little jock waiting near the end of the line to pay the entrance fee. In a few more minutes, the crowd would spill out onto La Brea. There was no question, tonight the place would be jamming. Regan grabbed Lynn by the elbow and escorted her inside, compliments of the house. Just last week Lynn had installed two telephone outlets in Regan's apartment, compliments of Ma Bell. It paid to have good friends. They always came in handy in a fix.

"O.K. ladies," Regan shouted, "Let's keep the line moving." Hardly were the words out of her mouth when someone caught her attention. Regan didn't recognize her at first because of the dark glasses, but upon closer inspection, she remembered the face. It was a hard face, but attractive all the same. The woman stood there, poised like a statue. Only this wasn't a marble statue, it was all steel. Rachel Mann was back in town.

You Look Like You Could Use A Light

Mercedes had disappeared like Eurydice into the bowels of the subterranean den. Crushing through the crowd of women, she made her way to the long narrow bar where Reva, the bartender, stood waiting to take her order.

"What can I do 'ya, doll face," Reva asked. She was a steady who had been tending bar on weekends for as long as Mercedes could remember. The rest of the week she was a Quality Control Inspector for Anheuser Busch. She was also a recovering alcoholic with the initials VSOP tattooed on her right arm. Reva, like the rest of her AA sisters, smoked an endless amount of cigarettes and drank cup after cup of coffee.

"Tanqueray and tonic. Better make that a double," she ordered, as she settled in to wait for Mona Lisa.

It was nearly midnight and the bar was packed with the regulars, the not-so-regulars and a few downright new faces, like the copper blonde next to Mercedes who sipped a strawberry daiquiri like a seasoned professional.

The terrain was completely familiar to Mercedes. The grey walls, the pink pelican wallpaper at the far end of the bar where black and white posters of Marilyn Monroe and Joan Crawford hung above a huge aquarium housing tropical fish; and in the center of the lounge area, on top of a small circular table draped with a dyed fisherman's net, the white-faced, lugubrious Morac danced to the seductive lilt of Sade's *War of the Hearts*. Holding a Corona in one hand and a cigarette in another, she appeared to be lost in the myriad gyrations of her body. She never spoke to anyone, at least Mercedes had never seen her do so. In between sets she sat at the bar and pushed limes in her beer. Women would buy her drinks and she'd nod her head, if she felt up to it.

Mercedes' eyes swept across the crowded landscape, coming full circle to the drink in front of her. The drink was lonely, so she gave it all her attention by polishing it off in a few gulps. Now that it was out of its misery, and she had nothing better to do, she slipped one of Reva's cigarettes from a half-empty pack. She started to caress the cigarette as she would a long lost love. A box of matches lay next to her drink.

At that exact moment, upstairs and almost directly overhead where Mercedes sat grappling with a guilty conscience--should she light up or shouldn't she?--a woman made her way down the flight of steps bordered by shards of mirrors.

They cast an accordion of her profile a foot in length and twenty-fold in depth. It was as if all the women she'd ever known and had ever been in her life, had assembled there that evening.

Mercedes sat at the bar, restless, distracted, and confused, her cinnamon cropped hair looking as though she'd been caught in a windstorm.

Then, suddenly, as if on cue, from out of the stairwell, shielded by the shoulders of the crowd, the woman, tall and dangerously self-assured, muscled her way through the cacophony of chatter.

"You look like you could use a light," a voice said behind Mercedes.

Mercedes whipped around and looked into the face of the raven-haired stranger. She was dressed in black, save for a leopard silk scarf draped around her neck and shoulders. It was twisted right above her heart and pinned in place by a striking quartz and emerald brooch, the kind your mother wore in the fifties, if she were that kind of lady. The kind who envied the real thing and thought she could get away wearing imitation jewels at a cocktail party. Only this didn't look like a fake.

"I don't smoke," Mercedes heard herself say, trying to hide the cigarette she still had in her hand.

"Looks that way to me," said the stranger, flicking a tortoise lighter right under her nose.

Mercedes dragged on the cigarette like a criminal reacquainted with a crime. For a second she thought of stamping out the cigarette, but took another drag instead.

"I'm Rachel. Rachel Mann," the woman said.

Mercedes said nothing. She was too busy staring at her. And she was definitely worth a stare. Her eyes were the color of seaweed; full lips demanded attention. Dark crimson, they appeared bruised, slightly swollen, as if too much blood had rushed to the surface. They were thirsty lips.

Rachel put on tinted, steel-rimmed glasses. "It's the lights," she volunteered. "My eyes are very sensitive."

Mercedes watched Rachel down a scotch and soda in the mirror above the bar. Rachel caught her stare. She threw back the rest of her drink, placed the glass on the bar and leaned close to Mercedes. She gave off a scent that was remote and foreign; an aromatic wet and dark, like a dense jungle in the midst of a downpour.

"You'd better stop staring at me," she teased. "I'm beginning to feel like a Christmas present." Rachel signaled to Reva to bring another drink.

Mercedes blushed. This woman was fast and smooth. Where'd she come from? Who was she? And how could Mercedes let her bully her like that and intimidate her into smoking?

Rachel looked down at her and grinned like they shared a secret no one else knew. Mercedes' stomach dropped. Her left foot had fallen asleep. She'd forgotten the taste of the first cigarette, so she let Rachel light her another. The woman was relentless.

"I could say, 'So do you come here often,' but that would be something you've heard a hundred times before. Anyway that's not your style. And I could ask you your name, but I already know that."

Mercedes looked surprised. Now both her feet were numb.

"And I could ask if you're waiting for someone." She took her drink from Reva. "But, yes, that's right, I know that, too." She placed a twenty on the bar and told Reva to keep the change.

"Well, since you know so much, maybe you could fill me in," Mercedes said, taking a big sip of her drink. Her head was spinning. Could Mona Lisa have sent her?

"We have a mutual friend. Her name's Mona Lisa and she's in a bit of hot water at the moment. I'm here to help get her out."

Mercedes was suspicious. "How do I know that?"

"Because I'm telling you, and I never lie." Rachel's words scratched the air like claws.

So much for stupid questions that went nowhere, thought Mercedes.

"She told me she'd be here by midnight."

"Seems like she missed her appointment. It's nearly one. I think she's tied up and can't get here."

"How do you know?" Mercedes questioned.

"Just a hunch," Rachel replied.

"How long have you known Mona Lisa?" Mercedes questioned, sipping her drink, all the while trying to keep calm, trying to show Rachel that she was in control. Only Mercedes didn't think she was doing a hell of a job convincing her.

"As long as anyone knows anyone in this town before they disappear. A couple of years," Rachel replied. Her eyes darted around the room like someone was pointing a gun in her direction, a double-barrel shotgun, only she didn't know where the trigger-happy assailant was staked out.

"Funny, she never mentioned your name," Mercedes said, hoping to catch the stranger in a slip.

"Mona Lisa has a habit of forgetting who her friends are. She doesn't realize we have her best interests at heart. She's mentioned your name to me."

"What did she tell you?" Mercedes was curious. From the corner of her eyes, she noticed Regan, arms folded, leaning up against the edge of the bar. The copper blonde who was fond of daiquiris, hung on Regan like a cheap suit. But Regan hadn't taken her eyes off the two women. Mercedes could sense she was burning up. Was it anger or jealousy or both? She suspected they knew one another, but they weren't going out of their way to be friendly.

Rachel didn't miss a thing. "I better put a helmet on. Regan's shooting daggers in my direction. I hope I'm not interrupting something."

Mercedes seemed embarrassed by the suggestion. She didn't want Rachel to think Regan had anything on her. Not that she did.

"Regan looks like that all the time," Mercedes kidded.

Rachel gave her a warm smile. "Not that I'd blame her. You're a very captivating woman. Mona Lisa was right. She said I'd like you."

"Not to change my favorite subject," Mercedes quipped, "but what's happened to her?"

Rachel avoided Mercedes' eyes. "All I can say for sure is that Mona Lisa's taken too much for granted. She had a bad habit of rubbing people the wrong way. And this time she went too far. There are people you just don't play with and Mona Lisa plays with everyone. And from the looks of it," she said, glancing around the bar, "you've been stood up, sister. Don't look so worried. I'll take care you get home safely."

That was the second time someone said that to her this evening. Mercedes suggested they go to Rachel's place for a nightcap.

Rachel looked pleasantly surprised. "You could be asking for trouble," her voice winked.

"What kind of trouble?" Mercedes replied, soon sorry she asked.

"The kind you look like you need," snapped Rachel, her eyes a crack of lightning as she gave Mercedes the once-over.

"Now what's *that* supposed to mean?" Mercedes questioned, glad to know the charm was still on ice.

"Anything you want it to," Rachel declared, slipping on a pair of black leather gloves. She gave it a few seconds, softened her voice and moved closer. "Seems to me you might enjoy it." Rachel blew the words in Mercedes' face like a cloud of smoke.

"Trouble?" Mercedes whispered, dizzy from Rachel's

warm, scotch-scented breath.

"What else did you have in mind?" Rachel asked, raising her eyebrows slightly as if the thought of anything else had never even occurred to her.

Mercedes took a deep breath. It didn't help. She needed to take about a thousand of them, but there was no time. Mercedes looked at Rachel--standing the five inches taller she always wanted to be—to see if she was nervous. But the woman was a cool cucumber. Mercedes couldn't put a finger on how she felt about her, but there was something fresh and wild about Rachel, something that made Mercedes wish she'd stick around longer than a hangover.

Hasta La Vista, Baby

Before Mercedes knew it, she was swept away in Rachel's black jeep, careening along Sunset Boulevard, jack-knifing around curves till the vehicle heaved up the faintly lit alleyway of the Chateau Marmont, just a few blocks from her home.

Mercedes checked herself in the mirror. Her hair was windswept, her cheeks rosy and her eyes glazed, but that had less to do with the night air and more to do with the booze.

She was vaguely conscious of gliding through ther small lobby, riding up an elevator and walking into a large, plush bedroom with a magnificent view of the Strip. Sure she was nervous, drunk and not entirely sure what to do with this beguiling stranger. Maybe she didn't have to do a thing.

Mercedes just stood in front of the window, weaving slightly, while Rachel ordered some food and drinks. Nothing to worry about, Mercedes thought to herself. Perfectly civilized, perfectly respectable behavior. They'd have a drink, have a nibble, and then she'd leave. Who was she kidding? Certainly not Rachel, whose conversation was more perverse than polite as she pressed her warm body against Mercedes' back. Where did she come from? Before Mercedes could figure out the answer to that question and before she knew what hit her, Rachel kissed her. It wasn't tender, and it wasn't rough. It was all possession. Erotic thievery; not very polite, but Mercedes fell for it. The sensation of the kiss split her heart. She couldn't breathe. Her temples started to throb, and she felt faint.

In a matter of a few seconds, the room went blacker than a crow. The walls started to close in on her. Then, without warning, the four walls fell back and the floor gave way and she plunged into a deep, dark pool. It had no bottom.

Mercedes felt herself flagged by thick ribbons whirling in concentric circles like the huge brushes of a car wash. She plummeted deeper and deeper into this bottomless pit. Then, just like that, she fell into Rachel's outstretched arms like a feather.

But she didn't stay there long. Rachel made her stand up and gave her a drink that tasted like a warm kiss. Mercedes obediently sipped the cool liquid while Rachel, smoking a thin Havana, marched around a desk over which a small, single-bulbed light was suspended. The room was full of smoke and fear and music. Somewhere in the distance, maybe over the rainbow, a lone sax, filled with heartache and remorse, bellowed the blues. The room grew warmer, glowing like a hazy sunset on a sultry summer's night. Only it wasn't the sun's radiation. It was an orange neon sign that flashed "Wet Dream." Where that came from was anybody's guess.

Rachel coughed to get Mercedes' attention. Then she tapped a pair of brown leather military boots on the tiled floor. She wasn't a woman to ignore, not in that get-up. She wore a skin-tight loden and khaki colored jumpsuit, part bounty hunter, part soldier. Maybe she couldn't make up her mind.

The one thing Mercedes could make out was the dance-card holder--polished, shiny and expensive--sitting on the desk. When Mercedes tried to grab it, Rachel slapped her hand with a riding crop. A woman like that could ride the wind out of an Arabian stallion, a water buffalo or a shark. Anything for the sport of it.

"Don't touch what doesn't belong to you," she commanded in a stiletto voice that cut to the quick. Then a smile, razor thin, slashed her face. She rang a bell. Mercedes thought it was nice of Rachel to serve supper, but what came through the door was nothing like beef stew, pasta primavera or a peach cobbler. It was a blonde--bad and beautiful--who didn't need an introduction. Wearing an outfit sweet and simple--a moire velvet black widow, thigh-high fishnets and pink slippers--Mona Lisa's devil-may-care face was partly obscured by a jewel-specked mask, and her sun-bleached hair fell wild and curly on her naked shoulders. She sat on the desk, crossing her legs with slow deliberation and leaned over to let Rachel kiss her. She paid no mind to her best friend.

This time Rachel proved her kisses could be tender. Mona Lisa moaned with pleasure. The murmur grew louder as Rachel started to caress her firm pale breasts which peeked out of the tight lingerie. Rachel's eyes, all treachery as she kept them pinned on Mercedes, were filled with a malicious glee only a bride stealing a husband from his childhood sweetheart could understand.

Mercedes' head was spinning and she broke out in a sweat. She started shaking from a cold arctic breeze sweeping across the room, blowing away all the smoke. Before she could say a word or move a muscle, the two women walked off with the antique and closed the door behind them. Their hollow laughter hung in the air like a witch's curse as they left Mercedes completely in the dark.

Mercedes bolted up in bed, but the sudden movement was

too much for her gin-soaked body. She looked around the empty room; a window had blown open, and the thin white curtains billowed like diaphanous wings of an angel. Only she doubted it was heaven she'd just visited. She'd been out cold. She tried to stay up but her head wouldn't let her. It was spiraling in that black pool of unconsciousness she'd just met for the first time and didn't particularly enjoy.

She felt like a negative waiting to be developed, and when the picture was clear, she didn't appreciate what she saw. Her sweater had been removed and so had her bra, but someone had been kind enough to leave on her pearls. That's not all they left. A bloodthirsty mark in the soft curve of her right breast was the sole imprint of a very arrogant mouth and the only evidence that any of this had really happened.

The pockets of her leather jacket had been turned inside out and her driver's license and photos placed on the table. So now Rachel knew where she lived, her weight, height and date of birth. She also knew Mercedes had the antique. The picture was gone, and so was Rachel. It all became clear now. How could she be so gullible? Mercedes wanted some answers, but the only answers she could conjure were Rachel's eyes, her smell, the kiss.

Mercedes turned over on her stomach and buried her face in the pillow. Her body quivered from rage, but then, little by little, she had to give in to the truth. Desire overcame her as her body pressed hard against the bed. All the time Rachel's eyes were on her, those lying, cheating eyes.

Mercedes' breathing was heavy now. Anger had given way to submission. She tried to fight it, but the more she did, the more she saw Rachel's eyes and remembered how those reprobate lips had bruised hers. And when she simply pictured Rachel's tongue stabbing her mouth, a final, violent breath expired from her, as the bittersweet name of Rachel echoed like a dangerous incantation in the silent night.

Terry Wolverton

each poem is a fist fight

each poem is a fistfight
kaboom! and the blood spurts
each word is a knuckle ready to bruise
just itching to rearrange my profile.

they don't fight fair.
sometimes they scratch,
pull hair, gouge eyes.
sometimes they pin me down
and won't let me up for weeks.

see this scar? these broken teeth?
I got 'em from poems, those bullies.
I'm not looking for trouble,
I'd rather hide like a coward under my desk,
but they come after me
grabbing me by the collar,
slamming me against the wall.

I tell you,
it's self-defense.

for Azul

she arrives at my house with a small box
I think oh a present, a gesture of love
I open it eagerly and find inside
three small blue feathers

and a hideous plastic toy, with bells
she says: that's all that's left
but it takes some time to connect the pieces
my little blue bird visiting her house
its cage atop the shelf, full of bells and seeds and toys
her dogs pacing below sleek and curious

she came home to find the cage on the floor
seeds splashed in every corner
the little blue bird on the dogs' bed
she says: she was pretty mashed
and bleeding
for me there is no corpse
just a small box with three stained feathers and the plastic
clown
no hound eyes panting up into my face
sorrowful at the death of their small toy
the end of the song

she cannot reach me in that moment
for I am spinning away like those small feathers
the bells in my head
remembering those hard little claws curling and uncurling
learning to trust the finger

she was cracking rocks with a hammer

she was cracking rocks with a hammer.
it took all the force of her will to shatter them
exploding earth eggs into universe
she was releasing the force of her will
to the four directions
she was smashing into what had been solid

breaking into bedrock, disintegrating
the compacted layers
she was killing her babies.
she was not censoring anything.
she was splitting the face of her existence
splintering her illusions
she was striking sparks
flinty and sharp-edged
she was using the tools as she knew how to use them
she was arching her arms
striking the blow
she was not being tender
moving stone to her intent
she was keen, she was intent
she was working her muscles
sweaty and fixed, making sand.

that poem you keep writing in your head, something about ice

about crawling out slowly over the ice
moving with great care across the frozen ledge
knowing that underneath is a terrible surge of water
you are moving to meet someone on the other side
although you cannot see it, you imagine it is verdant there
this draws you out
holding your breath, sliding your rigid trunk along
feeling your hipbones pressed against the diamond shelf
willing yourself to weigh nothing, like rime
still you hear the crack/the snapping of everything
you can't hold on you can't go back
can only plunge into the icy shock:

you are alone in a terrible surge of water
and either you swim
or you don't
the edge to cling to is melting under your reddened hands
and both shores are so far away.
it's not like you can climb out and up and into the bright sun
oh no
you must keep treading against the floes
to keep the heart pumping, to keep the blood from sleeting
to keep from becoming a glacier
and you will never reach the other side
will never be safe and dry
and you fear you will never never thaw.

I've been wondering why
it's so hard to see you

I've been wondering why it's so hard to see you
you tell me
you've been carrying me around in your pocket
that explains it
how cramped I feel, how cornered
rattling around like loose change
along with numbers collected on matchbook covers,
keys to locks that opened long ago,
and the dust of what's disintegrated
sometimes, absent-mindedly,
your hand slips in to feel me
not like the shiny apple that your fingertips savor
anticipating the biting in, the tasting
but rather like the rabbit's foot
you stroke for comfort and to bring you luck.

Judy Grahn

1960, Skeletons in Sergeant Kirk's Closet

SERGEANT KIRK WAS A LARGE, friendly, competent Caucasian woman, not sparkling, woody rather than brilliant or metallic, whose peppery black hair was only beginning to go to salt as she approached her middle years. She had made a career of being a noncommissioned officer in the Air Force, working her way up the chain of command from the bottom to the center. She had joined near the beginning of the establishment of the women's branch of the military, during World War II, when so many American women filled jobs that had traditionally been reserved for men. At least in our millennium, Sergeant Kirk (which is not her name) had many tasks in her responsibility as barracks supervisor for seventy women; she had many tasks and one obsession: Lesbians.

Sergeant Kirk had seen her share of official purges of Lesbians in the military, directed at eliminating the outspoken and daring, especially those who are dark-skinned but including plenty of white women too. She knew what could happen to the too honest and those unwilling to knuckle under to a man's definition of what women should act or look like. Though ostensibly aimed at removing "Lesbians," the purges are actually for the purpose of getting rid of "dikes," that is, the more independent women who have pride, intense loyalties, and strong, often romantic feelings about each other. One early veteran, Pat Bond, who was caught in the first wrenching, catastrophic mass arrest/interrogation program affecting thousands of American servicewomen on the eve of the victory of their army in World War II, knows how the persecution began. The purges began, she says, after the

American commanding general, General Douglas
MacArthur, watching the women soldiers disembarking in
Japan, said to his officers, "I don't care how you do it, but get
those dikes out of here."

So the "dikes," the ones who had been the first to break
with women's traditional roles, the more short-haired, muscular, intense, aggressive, passionate, and women-identified
of the servicewomen were suddenly arrested and charged
with the crime of Lesbianism. These women were humili-
ated, disgraced, isolated from society, turned against each
other in vicious police tactics of extracting "confessions" and
proof of guilt from their sister GIs, and bounced out of the
army they had served with loyalty and trust. They were left
without benefits, self-esteem, jobs, and all too often with
shattered family ties, since letters were sent to their parents
telling of the charges against them. Suicide, psychosis, fear
of sex, great mistrust of other women, lifelong terror and
bitterness were the fruits of the general's seemingly so casual
words "get those dykes out of here."

Sergeant Kirk had safely gotten through *that* big nightmare, and then the others followed with terrifying persis-
tence, sweeping over the intimate world of army bases every
few months with stern, repressive edicts from the highest
offices, accompanied by officers from the Office of Secret In-
vestigation (OSI), dressed in their FBI-type trench coats,
opening women's mail to search for innuendos of too much
affection, searching rooms for letters or photographs of
friends inscribed "with love," training women to act as spies
against each other, and conducting interrogations with no
lawyers or hint of prisoner's rights in an ongoing war against
women that no one talks about.

Sergeant Kirk did her job, gritted her teeth, survived these
cnditions, and learned to live with them by pretending that
she herself was different from the others. They were the

she would say, "even if it's a harmless-looking peck on the cheek, let me know at once. Lesbians can be very sneaky. Or if you see them holding hands, or spending a lot of time together. If you think someone is spending too much time in another woman's room, you let me know at once, because she might be a Lesbian." Women who would not turn another woman in were themselves suspected of being Lesbians.

Sergeant Kirk survived the purges against Lesbians accused of having sexual relations with each other and those accused of *maybe* having sexual relations, or *trying* or *planning* or *wanting* to have sexual relations. And when the military tightened still further, introducing the concept of "guilt by associations," meaning that anyone who associates with, is friendly to, spends time around, or even speaks to someone who is believed by the OSI to be a Lesbian is the same as a Lesbian, Sergeant Kirk spoke even louder and even more often about the nefarious evil and horrendous dangers of Lesbians in our midst.

On the other hand, Sergeant Kirk had the curious habit of breaking a cardinal rule prohibiting officers and enlisted drudges from seeing each other socially. This is called a rule against fraternization, brotherhood, though in this case, sororization, sisterhood, between the officer middle class and the enlisted working class is prohibited by the army as it is in the economic system. She liked to single out lowly and lonely enlistees who appealed to her, perhaps showed symptoms of boldness and intellectual curiosity (as most of us did), and take them to her room after lights out for a game of chess or even in her car to Church's drive-in on the highway toward San Antonio, for a hamburger and a Coke. She did this to me, and I was sometimes naively tempted to want to press her into admitting that she was really a dike underneath all that spy stuff. She had so many familiar mannerisms, a direct gaze, honest, emphatic hands, beautiful New England plain folk's speech. There was something romantic, almost sexual, in her warm eyes. But her remarks about recruits who were being suspiciously friendly stopped me from showing my hand. Since any break from the ugly boredom of barracks life was appealing to any of us, perhaps she just used these little illicit trips as a ploy or bribe to get more anti-Lesbian information. She made the same friendly overtures to another young woman, who years later and in a different part of the country became a friend of mine and told me parts of the sergeant's story I otherwise would not have known. Kathy Sparks, a tall nineteen-year-old enlistee with a very romantic nature, also went for hamburgers with Sergeant Kirk. She also told her nothing about Lesbians in the barracks since she was too inexperienced to know anything about sex or Lesbianism anyhow. But one weekend Sparks, like almost everyone who has recently entered the military, having no idea what was dangerous, fell into an even worse anti-Lesbian trap. The barracks were full of traps, for the OSI trench coat men had been busy and had developed a new weapon to ferret out the dykes in the army: decoy Lesbians. Earlier that year they had arrested another noncommissioned officer, a thirty-five-year-old sergeant who, like Sergeant Kirk, wanted a lifetime career. Sergeant Johnson had already been in for a decade and had worked her way up to recruiting officer, a pleasant job compared to some, when she was accused of Lesbianism. Confronted with the "proof" against her, she was given another choice. All charges would be dropped and she could stay in the service if she would serve as a spy and catch other Lesbians. She was to do this by using romantic entrapment as her method, and so she did. She invited the sergeant's new favorite, Kathy Sparks, to visit her on a ranch near the base, which was a training base in Texas. Sparks went, and the recruiting sergeant served her a nice dinner and wine, played soft music, and after a while began to make loving overtures

to her. When Sparks reciprocated, she was arrested for
Lesbianism, taken into custody, interrogated, and badgered
into signing a "confession." Her parents were then informed,
she was ostracized from the other women and finally dis-
charged three months later with a criminal record, no friends,
no skills, no self-esteem and no idea why this had happened
to her.

Then an unexpected thing happened. Sergeant Kirk had
an apartment in town, and she very quietly moved the devas-
tated Kathy Sparks into it. They began a strange, intense,
highly romantic relationship in which neither was allowed to
touch the other, even in the warm manner of friends. Sergeant Kirk brought her presents and flowers, using all the
tenderest language of love and affection, up to the point of
anything sexual. Sex was taboo. This continued for two
years, until Sparks was feeling emotionally well enough to try
again to venture into the shocking world by herself, and,
leaving the sergeant's care, she got a job in another city.

This is where I met her and heard of her strange affair
with Sergeant Kirk. There, although she became a top-notch
typist on a newspaper and had the possibility of putting
herself through college, for she was very quick, she suffered
instead from feelings that she had done a great wrong and
deserved punishment. She became a Tragic Figure, keeping
company with demoralized minor criminals who wore dark
clothes and had violent underpinnings. She often went to a
Lesbian bar in the city, and she had two lovers that she kept in
a state of rivalry, refusing to live with the one she had sex
with, refusing to have sex with the one she lived with. And
one night, in a deep fit of despair, she went into an alley and
beat her head savagely against a brick wall until she fell
bleeding and unconscious. When she was found in the morning, she told police she had been assaulted by some men.
And, of course, she had. She had been assaulted by the entire

government and its army two years before.

The story of her "beating" appeared in the paper, and she showed the article to her friends. "Just look at the sort of thing that happens to me," she said. She painted her apartment entirely in black enamel, ceiling and floor too, and she wore black clothing whenever she was off work. She did not recover from this period of her life for many years, although she later finished school and became a college teacher.

As for Sergeant Kirk, she completed her twenty years in the service and retired. She was given a big send-off and a pension and congratulated. She went home to a small town in Minnesota and stayed with her parents. On her first Christmas evening out of the service, having filled herself with liquor, the forty-year-old ex-sergeant climbed heavily onto the steep roof of her parents' home in the middle of the little town and stood knee-deep in the bitter snow. Then she removed every stitch of her clothing. For several hours she stood there, oblivious to all threats or pleadings, waving a shirt clutched in one hand, her face turned from the frozen earth as though signaling the fiery stars over her head, and bellowing at the top of her lungs, "I'm Gay! I'm Gay! I'm Gay!" And so she was.

Sharon Stricker

The Resistance

"We were never meant to survive"
these words of Black Feminist Lesbian poet Audre Lorde
sear into my brain like a branding iron on a cow's hide.

They are repeated by Native American Indian woman/
poet Joy
Harjo as she describes her Indian friend who escaped by
ducking from nine bullets fired straight for his head from
a speeding car. Says Harjo:

"We laughed at the impossibility and yet the truth of it.
Because who would believe the fantastic and terrible
story
of all our survival
those who were never meant to survive?"
Blacks
Native American Indians
Asians
Jews
Chicanas
Lesbians
Feminists
Women in Prison

We were not meant to survive.

And I think of you the storyteller
who will make her L.A. debut this Sunday reading

with me at Sisterhood Bookstore.
Two and a half years out of prison.

You are a survivor
You are a fighter
You will tell your own life
Penned through your new found voice and words

the fantastic and terrible story of it

the motherless and fatherless child
the wild one of five, reckless brothers and horse country wild
an Annie Oakley of this generation
shootin' from your hip
marryin' and bein' a good wife
Even Calamity Jane lost her baby girl
She became a drunk, a lush, a mean and ornery varmint

But she was a survivor.

Years and years of piling up pain/words

"You're a born whore"
"You're full of the Devil"
"I only have one daughter and she's the successful one"
"Don't tell or I'll kill you"
"If you love me you will"

words become daggers, become triggers, become knives,
become red blood, become venom, become rage, become
cancer,
become silencers, become silence.

Until you believe you are the bad seed, you are the crazy

you were never meant
                    to survive

You almost lose your mind locked behind shutters and
blinds
and motel windows that rob you of identity
just as he robbed you of your children

Where I met you was prison
on the last stop of the train for self-destruction
By then you surely knew you were not meant to survive.

But you did.
Through each one of these harrowing experiences
that tried to strip and rob you of your girlhood,
your motherhood.

You have become a warrior woman.
You are a fighter for survival.

This Sunday you will do your first
public reading outside of prison.

You were meant to survive.

Going too Far

   She says her real crime is alcoholism. That night in cold
December when she babysat for her acquaintance's three kids
she had thought, "Oh, good, they want to come over to my
house and watch videos." And she points her right index
finger to her brain and twists it like a switch and says, "To my
mind that meant, oh, good, I can drink."

She sits on the orange and yellow-striped couch across from me, hunched over in the black jacket she wears like a prison uniform. Endlessly she puffs on Camel filters. I could feel her frail body, like one of Modigliani's sad-faced women, screaming inside, "Just let me out of this prison."

"There are five girls threatening my life if I don't tell them my crime," she continues, her face red, her voice shaky. "They backed me up against the wall during Thanksgiving and said they were going to kill me. They wanted to see a paper guaranteeing my crime was forgery. I asked the lieutenant but he said they can't fake any papers. And you should hear the rumors. They say I molested little boys and cut off their penises." Her masked face cracked with a forced laugh as if to say how ridiculous and blown out of proportion this all was. I sat on the other end of the couch, stunned at the ugliness of the rumor, shocked that after all these years of working with so many women whose childhoods had been ruined by sexual or physical or emotional abuse, I was now discussing this crime with a woman. I had stopped working in the Men's Unit because I couldn't work with the men who were the molesters and the abusers at the same time I was working with the grown-up women they had abused. The dissonance in my brain, in my heart, in my body, caused a forest fire of friction. I could no longer tolerate the contradictions. I was pulled like a magnet, arms, legs, heart, mind, split and thrown out in two opposite directions.

Yet here the situation had come full circle. Before me sat a woman sentenced for being a child molester. Maybe she hadn't done it, but the courts had decided it was so. A six year sentence was not handed down lightly.

Yet who knew what really happened.

"I spent $50,000 on psychiatrists to find out," she continued. "I even asked them to do sodium pentothal so I could know for sure. That proved I wasn't lying."

"My crime," she reiterated, "is alcoholism. I know it. I started drinking years ago. I'd come home from work, and being a teacher I'd get home at 4 p.m. and start drinking then. My husband was so abusive and would beat me that I drank as a way to numb the pain. I thought no one knew. But it really got bad. I used to hide the Vodka bottles in the sofa, under the bed, wherever I could. I thought no one knew. Just like I thought no one knew about my husband's beatings. He's a guard at Folsom, you know. And I kept telling people, 'Oh, the dog bit me.' 'Oh, the kids at school accidently hit me with the ball in the yard.' Then one time my father, who's a doctor, was sewing up my lip and he said, 'Do you like it? Some women do.' And I said, 'No, I don't like it.' He said, 'Then get out.' The next week I filed for divorce."

"But by then my drinking was out of control, although I still went to work each day and drank at night. But I know I didn't molest that little girl while I was babysitting. My crime, my disease is alcoholism."

I listened sympathetically to her story. I learned with the men not to judge this crime. After all, only the other day a very sweet, bright, cheerful, Doris-Day look-alike except for her black skin had told me she'd shot her husband for his lying and cheating affair with another woman friend. Who is to say which crime is more heinous? I can never excuse the crime of child abuse. I know that this acting out is connected so deeply to a seething inner rage that comes from abuse that these women themselves have received as battered wives, as neglected or beaten children, as sexually molested or neglected young girls.

The violence against women comes full circle. The abused becomes the abuser. The victim victimizes. The suppressed rage surfaces. The cycle continues. The oppressed becomes the oppressor.

Women have barely begun to understand their rage.

The Blue Scream

Again today I met the woman of the Blue Scream
that Edvard Munch painting of a wild-eyed woman
with frenzied straw hair
atop a contorted putty-dough face
who cannot speak
who cannot scream
who buries her feelings until she is entombed
a walking prison
Hiroshima only a light match away.

    Five years and this image of a speechless woman
    predominates as the central key
    that unlocks the repressed rage
    that rampages through this women's prison.

        The pain of she who at 6 years old rose
        hungry and motherless each cold morning

        or she who at 9 ran like a deer
        homeless and scared out into the wind
        stumbling over broken shards of brandy and gin
        the stench of her parents' breath
        like the mad dogs beating

        or she
        the child in her white first communion
        dress of silk ribbons and lace
        long white stockings
        organdy sheer veil to her knees
        hiding shame at the sin
        of the old man who invited her in

and locked the door after.

and she at 14
who awoke all alone
in a pool of red blood
death she thought
as no parents had taught her
about pregnancy and protection.

Once again today she came to visit
in her grown up self
wearing her lavender eye shadow
and matching sweater
she sat on the couch at the prison and said
"I'm dying inside
I cannot cry.
Ever since October I have walled myself up
to not feel. I can't write.
I can't cry.
I can't create."

As I took her in my arms
and held her like my own child
I am reminded of you
who sat for 4 long months and barely
uttered a word till finally
you began to write:
    How Dave had rescued you at 15
    from a life of wandering and bars
    How you had loved him and given him
    two bright-eyed raven-haired daughters
    How he had broken your nose, your finger,
    your teeth, your pride.

You found your voice

You conquered the Blue Scream
You filled the balloon with words
not heroin
You shouted out the nightmare
of your rage.

    But let me tell you one thing
    Beware this Woman of the Blue Scream
    each season she emerges
    like tuberculosis from her grave
    and each time she comes
    she has no voice
    no words to say
    each time I see her glassy eyes
    and frozen fingers

    I must speak of you
    who found your voice that day
    you almost died
    you raised your voice like the clash
    of a 1000 cymbals poised to shatter glass.

Cradlesong

You cradle me in your arms and I tell you
        I am afraid of a hysterectomy
        how I know it's safe & 30% of the women
        have these fibroids but still
        it's scary
        like walking home in the late night dark
        down Broadway from a movie: no trees
        stirring

shadows moving
imaginary six foot men leaping out behind
grabbing me
no longer will I be whole.

You cradle me in your arms and say you'll love me
even when
my hair turns grey, my breasts are sagging
we'll grow old together
not to worry
you never loved me for my beauty
you distrusted blonde-haired, blue-eyed
goys.

You cradle me in your arms and I cry
I fear I'll be considered sexless
despised, rejected, repressed, ignored,
like the crones, the witches, the Hecates
in our culture.

Now I cradle you in my arms and begin
ever more
to love you
for what is happening here between us
is more than any hysterectomy could take
from me.

Bia Lowe

If It Happens During the Day

for T.W.

When the bombs hit will you be driving to work?
Will I have to climb onto the freeway
search every smelted steel box
until I find your hands?
I won't die right until I find your hands.

If I'm doing the shopping when it happens
I'd crawl through that smoldering swamp
past the mesh of wire racks, the truncated registers.
It won't matter that the money has blown all over,
the bodies of women pebbled with silver and glass.
It won't matter if my pants are body or my breasts exposed.
I'd hoist myself up once I reached concrete
and I'd know which direction would find you.

If this disaster drops like a wedge
into a day we can't undo,
and our bodies blaze up miles from each other,
it won't matter that the telephone has ruptured to bits,
power lines melting into pavement like crayon drawings.
It won't matter if we fought that morning.
I'd meet your gaze at that instant in spite of the distance.
I'd rise over this city like ash blown from a chimney,
and settle against you, and blot out the sun.
Insist the night is pulled snug around us
our stomachs together pressed into a psalm
the dark squared windows gleaming in their places
the cats asleep on either side.

October

To save us from wildness
they call us in from our games at dusk.
We trudged in and bowed our heads
while they closed their houses against the gloam.
The night, they said, has horns and hooves,
and will steal the souls of good children.
And like a bribe of candy,
they doled out Halloween,
one night's mischief,
contrived as wax teeth.

Yet while their cars slept
we set out
to reclaim the dark city.
Our eyes and ears resumed their large shapes.
We remembered how to howl,
how to bare our teeth,
and the streets returned to river rock.

Now on Hallow's Eve
we lie on my living room floor,
our heads in the open doorway.
The drone of the freeway dissolves
as we look up past the oak —
some stars are brave against the city's bubble.
An owl calls.
These spirits endure.
We, too, are here.

A Kind of Witness

No sound in the eye of that storm,
just a sudden bright picture of death.
Everywhere lightning struck,
but without thunder.

Further out, where the roar hit,
winds shredded the city
and drops of rain
big as dogs' eyes fell.

People and animals did the best they knew how,
stepping over sign posts,
heading for the river.

Days later, flesh found an answer.
Too stupefied to mend right,
bodies fell into revolt,
and wounds hung open
like the windows of abandoned houses.

Forty years later, I remember the part about the eyes
    that had melted,
that had changed forever
in that last vision of heat.
They became a kind of grieving
and ran down the face, falling in drops,
aimless as spilled water.

And I remember the part about the river
that boiled up into the night like an open vein.
And how the people who sought comfort in the water

once wet, felt their flesh unfasten.
Some stood, knee deep,
their skin hanging like unfamiliar clothing
their arms outstretched like scarecrows,
voiceless in the fog.
That red fog, I won't forget.

And especially I remember a film
with women kneeling.
In a slow dream their arms swept across their hair.
It was gathered like the stalks of plants
whose roots had rotted. Whisked,
without effort, into piles.

A Poem about Two People Suspending a Balloon in the Air with their Breath

It used to be then, in her apartment in Echo Park, she would touch you and the back of your eyes would start swimming with toys. And almost always before your orgasm you would see very brightly colored plates, cups and saucers. Her room would fill up with cups and saucers. Tangerine, lemon, cherry, lime. And toys like tops or slinkies or letter blocks would tumble down the sheets. The cat didn't seem to mind. Her purrs were tiny motor boats, sailing out the bedroom window toward the lake.

That Spring you were happy like a child, the way you hadn't been happy as a child.

You were a child, convinced of the supernatural and fully expectant. Like a child you knew how statues come alive, how spirits speak through the bodies of animals, how trees are eager to help lost children. You were both that way together, making your way through an animated garden.

Then things began to change. Now trees are for shade, animals for companionship. Statues are for decoration, period. Now you know about the shadows in that garden. Wicked shadows that swallow children too eager for magic. All adults know this. So you have both grown older together, safe from enchantment. Safer, older.

And now I'll tell you something--when you grow old enough you'll understand why sex is obscene. It's like quicksand, too late before you realize the danger. Years later you'll remember the way her eyes closed before her lips parted. Even the memory will drag you under.

Trust is the obvious issue here. Like jazz. Everything depends on the two of you at that moment. Even more perhaps like poetry, like a poem about two people suspending a balloon in the air with their breath. The poem is the skin of the balloon, with breath pressed against all sides of it—that tense, that hoped for. Something tangible bobbing above you. A trace of your aspirations. And you know that like jazz, like poetry, it's just compensation for repressed religious tendencies. The two of you diving into bed, hoping for heaven, praying for a less culpable glimpse of nature. Struggling for humility.

And don't tell me, I know what a frightening struggle that is! Once you've let your guard down, forget it! She'll change you forever. You'll bite into her neck and like the taste of her blood. The sound of your paws pacing in the night will alarm the neighbors downstairs. Your tongue will hang shamelessly in public places and your mother will disown you.

Sex is a bag race, a bowl of sashimi, a familiar pair of shoes. And obviously like dancing--the way too much thinking can make you clumsy, the way sentiment can give you grace. A chance for everyone to star in a musical. A way to make good.

On the other hand, it's everything taboo. It teeters above the unknown, a roller coaster with a cracked rail. Flirtation with death, madness, possession. Worst of all, it's cannibalism. Wanting to chew your way through her windpipe, gobbling up the smell of her breath. Mouthing the insides of all her guts. And to be fair, you too want to be eaten. You beg to be served up like the most delectable sacrifice. Lucky for you she's starving. Unlucky for you, there's a limit to this appetite.

So some day it's over, the bag race is run, the magic is spent. There was something unnecessary about all the torture--you still hang on smiling with pie on your face. Because, let's face it, sex is comedy. A banana peel on every step. Two clowns making embarrassing noises, shoes so big they get caught in the sheets. She bites your round red nose, you respond by honking your horn. In the end you're crying with how much you have laughed. You walk away alone. You won't forget the smell of her ears.

S.Diane Bogus

MAYREE

Have you seen her? Mayree?
Comes decked in a black, crepe dress, Mayree.
Stands centerfold and shouts loud, Mayree.
The biggest woman in the crowd, Mayree.
Have you seen her? Huh, have you?

Red gardena in her hair, maybe.
Red gardena on her breast, Mayree.
Most ample and out of breath, Mayree
From honky-tonk struttin', Mayree.
Have you seen her? Have you?

Black lace hanky in her hand, Mayree.
Rhinestones shine—her wrist and neckbands, Mayree.
Silk-stocking, T-strap, spiked heeled, Mayree.
Doing exactly what she please to feel, Mayree
Misbehaving, party-raving, Our Soul saving, Mayree!!
Tell me, have you seen her?

Ah, switching, bitching, belly-booty-bumping, Mayree,
Shaking thumping, round and round her rumping, Mayree.
Heard a fella shout, "Get down, Big Mama, Mary!"
Had to put that fella out; we don't know no **Mary**.
It took years to make our stout, blues mama, Mayree
And I wonder, have you seen her?

THE CREATOR'S DALLIANCE
Psalm 4
(Madam Booker T. Einstein Houdini Curie)

How magical a Maker is my God.
How inventive a maker is She.
How completely, fully, genius
a maker is my God.

He seized an un/none moment;
yes, She did suddenly seize the time;
stopped Her Being to Become,
stopped His Being to Become
less than none more than one.
She seized and made the time.
O celebrate Her Beingness, His
willingness to be;
use His voice, you, everyman,
can't you feel you're She?

O celebrate the face you have;
celebrate the eyes, the nose,
the cheeks, the chin, the brain,
the lips, the teeth, the neck, the rest,
the body whole remains.

Think you, would you, were you God,
have thought to first make face?
Would you, were you, could you, God,
invent, in flavors, race?

Then, exalt ye, exalt ye, exalt ye all
all faces, alone, in crowds;

exalt the ugly, dark, the blurred,
the pretty, light, the scarred.

How magical a maker is my God;
how imaginative is He,
to invent faces for her Selves,
to think up face all by Himself,
to zap up face and face again,
to mix up faces and match the skins,
to do it time and Time again,
and convince us that
they're *ours*.

SMALL TIME PROFUNDITY #2

As I sat down,
The old, lady waitress
asked
"Is someone joining you, dear?"
No, I nodded sadly.

When she returned with the coffee,
hands shaking as she served,
I had the controllable urge to ask:
"But would you?"

LADY GODIVA

As hope I bid you dream of her
Astride her ivory stallion
Arriving bare, with breasts for you,
Upon some wide, green galleon.
Leaning down she will offer you
Cho-co-late and a fantasy ride—
Look lusty, lustful, hot for you
Her voice a piper's, pied.
You climb behind her butt, her back
A back that's brazen to behold,
Touching her, your pubic hair
Sparks that that's wanton in your soul.
She laughs aloud, gives sex full reign
To her brilliant, strapping horse.
It rears, her smell wafts all about
Fragrant, moist, then off—
"Lady Godiva, Lady Godiva,
I fear, I want, I need!"
She laughs again, rides on as fine
With all of passion's speed.

Both new and young to bareback rides,
As new as much to self,
You clutch at first, her waist, her breasts
Then grip her thighs' deep cleft.
Seasons of smell, years of taste
Spread out beyond, headlong
She rides, you ride, she rides,
You ride, you ride, she rides you on.
La dy go dive a la dy go
Dive, the horse's hooves lay rhyme.
Up and down and up and down

She rides you out of your Mind.
To places untouched, reds unfelt,
To blues, the hues of come.
She knows the way to Orgasma Hill
The knoll where she was born.
Lady Godiva, Lady Godiva,
Enchanted Princess Charm
Lesbian of dreams undreamed
I offer her now as one.
Should you go there, should you go
Where I spin the way for you

Go again when alone in bed;
Go, whenever you do.
Lady, go dive a lady ...Go
Dive a lady, go dive
A lady...go dive a lady

Jess Wells

AQUA

I'D NEVER SEEN ANYONE looking so relaxed and content, her cowgirl boots propped on a chair-back, face pointing up to the blistering sky as if waiting for a kiss. Her jeans were tight, her shirt unbuttoned to the middle of her chest, and she was so long and stretched out that I didn't want to disturb her, but I had car trouble and in the middle of the desert you don't have many choices.

"S'cuse me," I said, stepping onto the wooden porch. "Wouldn't you know this piece of junk'd be having problems and me in the middle of nowhere with no money and nobody to call. I don't suppose you'd have any ideas, would you?"

I didn't have any reason to be explaining my financial business to this woman, but somehow my mouth forgot all about privacy that day. I should have seen from the response I got that it was time to back off the porch and leave. She slowly turned her head and opened her eyes, little green slits in a face that had been taut for the sun, but was now wrinkled and parched as it surveyed a sweaty traveler on the steps. I know not to poke at spiders, even the harmless ones, but I proceeded anyway.

"My car's acting up. Is there a station near here...or a phone?"

"Nope. Neither of those, but you can sit down if you want. We got a birthday party here," and she turned her face back to the sun.

I crossed the eight-foot porch, stood at the wooden chair beside her.

"But don't sit on the hat," she mumbled.

I scowled at her.

"You know about cars?" I asked, picking up the cowgirl

hat and, finding no place suitable for such a gem, snapped it into her lap. I sat. She turned, sensing the challenge, and plopped her hat on one of the railing posts.

"What's the trouble?"

"I'm losing power. She's not good for much, this car, but every few minutes she gets slower and more tired, then she picks up speed again."

"It's from the heat."

No joke, I thought. I considered leaving, trying to ignore how worried I was about the car or how much I hoped she'd offer me something to drink. Everything was from the heat, as if the sun were making us all water drops in an oily skillet. Everyone I had talked to today was irritable and short, things popping out of their mouths that belonged miles away from their minds. How she could sit there staring up at the sun was more than I could gather. I was ready to dash into her house uninvited and drink anything I could find.

"Park it behind the house to cool down. Relax. She'll be all right after the sun goes down a bit. Your radiator all right?"

"I don't know. I'd be surprised if it was. Whose birthday?"

She put her feet down and turned to me, stroking sun-blonde hair from her forehead. "Sorry, I'm not really unfriendly. I get like a lizard in this heat—just bake in the sun and forget everything. It's mine. My birthday." She got up and went into the house.

"Congratulations! So, do you live here year 'round?" I called after her.

"Yeah. You want some ginger ale? It's all the party favors I got."

"Love it. What is it today, 95, 100 degrees?" I asked, feeling the sweat running down my cleavage.

"Hundred and two." The refrigerator in the house moaned

against the battle of being opened. She handed me a tall glass with ice and bubbly. The ice shattered and scurried around inmy glass as I took a long swallow.

"You traveling alone?" She stretched out and looked straight ahead, the lines in her face deep and dry.

"Always."

She grunted her approval.

"My name's Jody. Thanks for this," I said, saluting her with the half-empty glass. "So where's all the party guests? Am I the first?"

"My name's Aqua," she toasted, without looking away from the sun.

"That's your name? I mean, aren't you a little far from home?" I laughed. I should have quit right then, I know that now, but the porch was shady where I was sitting and I would have pawed the ground for another glass of ginger ale.

"I was thinking about that just as you came up, actually." She turned to me. "Born in the sea. No point in staying."

"No point..." I muttered. Looking back on the day, I can see what I was doing: picking and poking, bearing down like the sun had been doing on me all day.

"I told you," she was getting annoyed. "I was born there. You know," her voice went low and conspiratorial, "it's like trying to stay in your momma forever."

Dyke, I thought. Our eyes met. Only a dyke calls a car 'she' and talks about being born.

"I like the ocean, actually. The breeze, the smell of it, the constant pounding..." I said, confused, wishing the ocean would pour around my miserable body instead of this puddle of sweat sitting on the shelf of my belly and this sand chafing the back of my neck. "I'm talkin' about a nice cool dip in the water."

"I hate the ocean," she said brusquely. "Had enough of it, anyway, that's for sure." She leapt out of her seat, alive

suddenly, her mind waking up, her energy running up and
down her long body in a torrent.

"Think your car's cooled down," she said through clenched teeth. "We could check her radiator. Maybe tighten a few
belts." She went into the house for another ginger ale.
"Never mind. You still thirsty?" I followed her.

"Yeah."

"How about bourbon in this one?"

I nodded.

"Oh, now I'm coming alive. Christ, who can think in that
sun. Besides, I don't get a lot of company--not many women
travel alone and even fewer come through here." She handed
me my glass and looked at me. "Not women like you,
anyway."

"Like us, you mean?" I said. She just snorted, stared into
her bourbon with a splash of ginger ale. "Whaddaya do out
here--for work, I mean?" I said.

"I'm a dancer in Reno. One of the big clubs--not strip,
mind you, I'm a dancer. I throw everything I've got into
every piece of music, so I'm good."

"Sounds great, Aqua," I said in a lack-luster tone. There
was something missing in the way she said it, like a birthday
party with no guests.

"It's life to me, you know, the joy and beauty of it all, set
to music. I tell 'ya, Jody," she said, with a dead-pan face,
"there's nothing like it. Life just leapin' and jumpin' all over
the place. Hey, bottom's up."

"To life," I said.

"Yeah. I'll go for that. And you? You gotta work?"

"I work with kids. Preschool in San Francisco."

"Oh, now, that must be something. Little ones. Damn'd
if life isn't glorious, you know?" She smiled but her eyes
never changed, still little green slits with no sparkle.

"Most of the time, I suppose," I said, looking into my

glass.

"Ah, all the time, honey. Just when things get bad at work, somebody gives me attitude or the place gets so smoky it makes me sick, well, just then I'll be driving home, tied up in knots, and there's the sun rising and it looks so...so," and she blew a half-kiss to the air, trying to explain joy to me with the broken face of someone watching their only chance at love drive away.

"You know what I mean?" she said.

"It must be really beautiful around here," I said, following her back outdoors.

"Oh, it is. I love the dust and the sun and the way the wind smells so dry out here. People think just because the sun shines all the time that the weather's always the same but they're crazy. There's spring sun different from winter sun and the flowers--you really have to know where to look to see them. Cactus, birds, the clouds. And the hills? They're solid rock and they look different, too. Even the dunes--you saw them a couple of miles south, right?"

"Yeah. Beautiful."

"All the tourists go to the dunes. Well, even *they* have seasons and there ain't nothin' grows out there." She took a long swallow. "Flowers are just a lazy way to tell the seasons, anyway. Makes me happy to think all this grows without water."

I looked at her with a long and steady gaze until she turned to me and her face seemed to close up again. She reached down and pulled at my glass.

"Time for a refill."

I shrugged my shoulders and let her take my glass back into the house.

"We got us a little party goin' on here, huh?" she called, dropping in more ice. "Well, good," she kicked the screen door open and handed my glass over my shoulder. "I don't

drink, really. I've had this bottle for a long time, but what the
hell. Today's my birthday and...it's nice to have company."

"So Happy Birthday," I said, raising my glass. "How old
are you?"

"Sixteen," she said, flopping into her chair.

I laughed. "So when did *you* stop counting?"

"I said, I'm 16," she leaned over the arm of her chair,
grave and threatening.

"Well, you don't *look* 16," I said, trying to diffuse the
situation by touching the deep crows-feet around her eyes.

"Hey," she pulled away violently. "I said there weren't
many of you women traveling through, I didn't say there
weren't *any.* "

"Sorry," I said, setting my glass on the chair and holding
up passive hands.

"Yeah, well, I'd say you should keep that glass between
your legs, girl."

"Is that so? Well, I imagine you'd be as frosty if you were
there."

"Oooh, now, I don't have to be this friendly. You could
just get in your car and scald, you know." She plopped her
feet on the railing, then sighed and turned back to me.

"Oh, I'm sorry," she said, shaking her head. "But dammit, it's my birthday. Sixteen years ago I was born from the
sea."

"Aqua," I said, feeling brave from the drink.

"All right, all right. It's the anniversary of my mother's
death," she said, lowering her voice. "You want another
drink?" She got up, quite drunk now and groped into the
house, came back with both bottles under her arms. "Save
some energy and just bring 'um out here, hell."

"I'm sorry about your mother," I said softly, fearing thin
ice.

"What for?" she asked, quietly, twisting open the ginger

ale. "She had a choice."

"She killed herself?" I felt sick inside, knowing I was prodding a lizard that had hissed its last warning.

"Yep. She sure did. Nearly killed me and my little sister with her. Did kill my little sister."

She wiped sweat from her forehead with her sleeve. "I shouldn't be so hard on her, I suppose. She had a bad time of it. Two kids, one always sick--my sister was such a weak little thing--and no man around, though when he was, it was worse than when he wasn't, of course. She was a grill cook. We lived in a little town by the ocean. You know, same old story."

"Work to pay the bills but the ends don't meet so you work some more and they still don't meet?" I asked sympathetically.

"Yeah. Well, one day she couldn't do it anymore so she put on her best sweater and pants, strapped my sister to her chest with the tablecloth and grabbed me by the wrist. Marched us on down to the sea. You don't want to hear this."

"Well...I do if you want to tell it," I said cautiously.

"She stood there for hours, looking at the water and nothing could move her. Her face didn't change. Not once. I know 'cause I watched her. I think maybe she'd taken a bunch of pills or something because I've never seen anybody so unreachable, you know, their face miles behind their flesh. So, we're standin' on this cliff and I keep going, 'c'mon Mom, let's go home now. What's the matter, Mom? We better go--you gotta cook in the morning.'" She looked down at her boots, then out toward the desert.

"Well, Happy Birthday, Aqua."

"I guess I was about eight, ten. Anyway, she never looked at me, just all of a sudden hiked me onto her back and dove off the cliff onto the rocks."

"Jesus Christ," I said, setting my glass onto the porch.

"Oh now, don't go all dramatic on me. It was a short cliff.
Maybe about six feet up. Can you believe that? I mean,
why'd she pick a place like that? My little sister, she died
right away. She didn't know what was going on and she sure
was too small to make up her own mind, but me, I clung to the
back of that sweater like it was the edge of the world. I guess
when we hit, I rolled off and I just lay there, on the top of the
rocks."

"Oh Aqua, I'm really sorry."

"Real flat ones, like shelves out into the water, with
crevices running through them. So I'm flat on my belly--I
didn't want to look towards Mom, and I was thinking, 'You
better hurry up and die before the tide comes in.'" She
snorted, taking another long pull on her drink. "Pretty weird,
huh?"

Aqua got up from where she was slumped over in her
chair and walked to the end of the porch, leaning her forearms
on the railing and kicking at the sand piled up around the
posts. She finished her drink and poured another.

"I remember everything--every single thing--about that
night. It's like I can still feel the stone against my belly and
the coldness. Must be because it's my birthday but I can see
that water surging up, waving the green slime back and forth,
saying, 'get out'a here girl, leave now, you've seen enough,
now go!'

"It started gettin' dark so I got up and didn't ever look
over at my mother, I just went straight to the cafe and told 'em
what happened and they took me in. Mrs. Miller put me in
her house behind the cafe and put me to work washing dishes,
but I don't remember much about being there. It's like my
mind went blank until the day I ran away and swore I'd
celebrate life always." Aqua strode across the porch and
clinked glasses with me. "Yes m'am. Celebrate."

"Oh hell, there, traveler Jody, don't look so sadfaced,"

she laughed with a crooked smile, quite drunk. "Everybody makes their choices: she chose to die and I chose to live and that's that. No regrets, goddammit," she said, pouring another drink into her half-full glass. "I say life's burden enough without carrying around a lot of sadness. Here's to it, honey--lightening life's burden. To dancing!"

The sun was finally going down and the desert was lit up behind her. As Aqua leaned on the railing, she looked on fire, like the sand.

"Mamba, rumba, salsa," she twisted and spun in her boots, laughing with her mouth, but her eyes still tiny and expressionless. "And of course square dancing and the two-step: I even know Czechoslovakian folk dances--pretty, real pretty. You should come see me dance, Jody."

"Great. I'd...like that a lot," I said, heavy and frightened.

She yanked open the screen door with a laugh and stumbled inside, turning on lights. I followed her into the tiny house and went to the sink to rinse out my glass. I'd had half the number that she had downed, but another drink and I'd never be able to drive: I was already counting on the freeway being a straight away through the desert. I turned on the water, feeling it cool and refreshing across my wrists.

"What are you doing?" Aqua said, alarmed.

"You don't have to play hostess, I can...."

"Turn off the water!"

"What?"

"Turn it off!" she shouted, stumbling across the cabin towards me. "I don't like it...water...in my house. It...makes the place smell."

I turned to Aqua, who was deliriously drunk, leaning over the back of a chair, looking down at the plastic-covered kitchen table.

"Damp. I hate it. Everything was so damp, Jody, my little bed behind the cafe, the air every day. Every single fucking

day was wet," she said, and I, parched despite the drinks,
standing there gritty and sandy and covered with dried sweat,
looked at her as if she were talking about the moon.

"The salt all over my body from lying in the water, the
lichen...in my nose, on my cheeks, green and...wet.
Little...things swimming in the tide pools." She turned her
head in disgust and staggered backwards. I wiped my hands
on my dusty pants and grabbed her by the shoulders, leading
her to her iron cot against the wall where she slumped onto
her side, face twisted and closed, knees to her chest, hands
like dried claws. I grabbed one of her feet to take off her
boots.

"I swear to you, I can still feel it, Jody. Her sweater."

I took off her boots, and as the sand poured out onto the
floor I looked at this woman, all parched skin and rough
hands, passed out in her dusty house. I thought of my own
mother, baking cakes she never ate, wringing her hands while
she stared out the windows at nothing, and I knew there was
no running from the pain of knowing that your mother may
never be happy. I set the boots beside her and fished in my
pockets for the keys. Feeling helpless and withered, I quietly
closed the screen door behind me and, touching the sand on
the railing as if willing it to protect her, I got in my car and
drove.

Carolyn Weathers

CRAB APPLE SUMMER

CRAB APPLE SUMMER was one of the hottest summers the rolling prairie ever had. By the last day of school, the pink and white spring blossoms, that had been so sweet, were shriveling on the ground. By June, summer was deep green and shimmery. Grown-ups fanned themselves, tinkled ice cubes in their big tea glasses and said August was bound to be a scorcher, perish the thought.

I was ten and didn't care about August, so far off, and heat. School was out. I threw my shoes into my bicycle basket and raced home barefoot, to freedom, hoping Miss Cross was watching from her classroom when I did it. At recess during school, Tommy Beasley and I used to take off our shoes and go barefoot, and one time Miss Cross stamped up to me and said: *Jane Jones! You put your shoes on right now, young lady!* I asked how come Tommy didn't have to. She said because Tommy was a boy and his feet were tougher. Now I knew that wasn't so. Tommy and I had just raced each other across the school yard, and my bare feet flew over the ground, while Tommy mostly hopped straight up, because the pebbles were bruising his tender feet. I put my shoes on, all right, but when Miss Cross left, I took them right back off again.

I raced home on my bicycle, glad more than usual for summer vacation, because I had shamed myself at school that last week, because of my overweening pride--as they call it in Sunday School.

Summer days were bright blue and hot, made-to-order for inner tube fights at the pool and diving underwater for Crackerjack toys, with our open eyes stinging from chlorine. My

big sister, Diane, was twelve. On hot, honeysuckle nights
we'd play Flying Statue and let ourselves land in whatever
pose we wanted, maybe a swan dive or a chair, and only
pretend it happened by chance. Later on, inside the house,
Daddy swept across the living room, reciting, "The Crema-
tion of Sam McGee," hoping the sound of all that ice and cold
would help. Mother made lemonade and dabbed our sun-
burned noses with sour cream. Sometimes she'd sing something as nice as she was, in her high voice, like, *Carolina
Moon,* or *Toyland.* After Diane and I had listened, we'd
plead for her to sing, *Hard-hearted Hanna, the Vamp of
Savanna, G.A..* And she'd roll her eyes and sing it.

Summer got hotter and shimmered out in front of us. All
of us kids were calling it Crab Apple Summer by now,
because we had never seen so many before. Look up, and
there was a crab apple tree, stuffed full. Look down, and
there were crab apples all in the grass. We used them same
way as Easter eggs--to throw at each other or to chonk at trees
and garter snakes. Mother got peeved at me when I came
home from Tommy Beasley's birthday with crab apple splat-
ters on my party dress, and after she had made me promise
her I'd act like a little lady. But I just could not act like one
for more than two minutes, before the urge to tear around
took over.

Crab Apple Summer was crammed like any other, with
foot races, bicycle expeditions and playing Superman. Up
Henderson Street, in the vacant lot, a bunch of us neighborhood kids, girls and boys both, played baseball till dusk, till
the lightning bugs blinked on, and it was time to go home for
supper. I'd hardly know what I was eating sometimes, for
remembering the thwack of the bat against the ball when I hit
it really good and could watch the ball fly high into the
neighbor's yard; or for remembering the good spray of dirt
and smear of it on my jeans when I slid into home.

When we got tired of playing what we'd seen at the

Saturday afternoon movie, like The Three Musketeers with
garbage can lids for shields and paper sacks for helmets,
Diane, Tommy, Pat Wheeler and I had wrestling matches in
the back yard. One magic night that summer Daddy took us
into Fort Worth for the real live wrestling. Diane even caught
one of Gorgeous George's golden hair pins, that he threw out
to us peasants. Diane kept it in a matchbox, one we were
going to bury a turtle in, but we just wrapped the turtle up in
some of Mother's wax paper and kept the matchbox for the
golden pin. Sometimes, at night, we'd sit in bed, real quiet,
and she'd hold the golden pin up to the moonlight ladder at
the window. Her eyes would look into some magical distance; I could feel mine doing it, too, and we'd dream dreams
and make wishes on the pin. Later, she lost the golden pin,
and it kind of went the way of the Tooth Fairy. But we got
where we didn't need golden hair pins to dream or wish right
or learn that wishing by itself didn't make it so.

I loved moving around, how it felt, the swing of it, the
way my muscles let me jump, roll, hop, run, twirl, stop short.
I loved how the world looked through the leaves and branches
of a high tree. And Mother and Daddy didn't care how red in
the face I got from playing, either. It was Miss Cross at
school who'd make me sit on the dunce stool after recess and
make me be an example of what happened if you played too
hard; you turned scarlet, that's what you did; and a girl, too.
But I was proud to be scarlet in the face from playing hard.

Another thing we did that summer was play badminton in
the backyard. We'd be going to church camp later on that
summer, end of July, and Diane was up for her fourth year as
camp badminton champion in the intermediate division. If
she won, she'd get a big gold plastic trophy from Brother
Williams' hardware store that I'd helped pick out, with lots of
goop and doodads on it. I was proud she wanted to practice
badminton with me. I was that good a player.

In the middle of Crab Apple Summer, before the river and

Biggers Pond, all of which happened in the last half of summer, my pride got overweening again. It was a night so warm and still, you could hear moths batting against the yard lights. Aunt Eloise and Uncle Jerry, and some grown-up neighbors, were sitting in lawn chairs, eating the ice cream Mother and Daddy had cranked up. It was time for the acrobatic show. I was first and cartwheeled from behind the crepe myrtle tree, fast as a cat, then flipped onto my feet and onto an empty oil barrel, which I rolled around the yard, forwards and backwards, by running on top of it, balancing and doing my feet just right. Oh, it was glory to hear those oohs and ahhs and all that clapping. When my turn was over and Diane started her act, I didn't like it--just standing there, watching and being polite.

She was getting more oohs and ahhs than I did. She was doing great and wonderful things, like swinging high on the swings by her feet. It was awful. My sinner's pride caused me to grab a hoe from the garage and bound across the yard with it, crossing between the show-off Diane and her admirers. It caused me to try and pole vault over the hedge with that hoe, only I didn't vault high enough and went smash into the middle of the hedge. I was wedged in there so tight it took four grown-ups to pry me out. They were real cross about it, too, and couldn't figure out what made me act so rude and crazy. *You sit down there, Jane Ellen, and behave*, they said, *and let your sister finish her show*. So I squatted down and glared at Diane, as she, to spite me, glorified herself more than ever doing flips on the swing ropes.

We went to the river that summer, too. The Puloxi River was brown, wide and smooth. It smelled like clay from its banks, and grapevines overhung it. Diane and I swung from these vines into the river. I was always Boy or Gorilla, never anybody important like Tarzan, who was always Diane, because she was older. When we played Tarzan at home, Betty Bennet, who was twelve, like Diane, was always Jane. She and Tarzan got to go off and play house in their tree. It seemed funny to me that they would not let me--Boy--come, too, but I wasn't invited, and that's how it was.

Diane got her toe caught by a snapping turtle, out by a rock in the river. She tried shaking it off, but the turtle didn't finally let go till Daddy pointed a lit match to its face. Diane inspected her toe and said: *I'm going to get that turtle; wait and see.*

That night, to help heal Diane's toe, we had a scrumptious supper: pork and beans and Velveeta cheeseburgers. Wood smoke mixed with river smells. Night animals, frogs, bugs scrambled in the dark; they creaked and croaked their conversations. Later, deep at night, Diane and I lay on our cots under a sky so starry it looked like black velvet with holes punched in it, and on the other side was the biggest star in heaven shining through every pinpoint punch. We were very quiet. We each now had a shame, and we each one knew we were thinking about it.

After the acrobatic show in the backyard and before church camp, something awful happened to Diane. She sat up in the walnut tree all day and said she would never come down, she would not let this happen to her, she refused for it to, so there! Daddy told Mother, *You should have told her,* and Mother said, *I know, but she's barely twelve.* Diane climbed down from the tree after it got dark, and whatever it was she wasn't going to have, she had anyway, just like she couldn't get that snapping turtle off her toe by shaking it off.

She was so mad about the tree business, she couldn't think about much else. The very next week at church camp, she lost the badminton tournament--and lost it to Tommy Beasley, who strutted around enough to turn your stomach. I was supposed to act nice, but it took some effort. The church had an ice cream party that night, and for a consolation prize Diane got her ice cream piled skyhigh with extra nuts, cherries and four kinds of topping. Diane smiled and thank you'd through her grit teeth. After a few bites, she gave her ice cream to me. I ate it all, and when Tommy Beasley was watching, I spooned it up so deliciously that he looked ready to give me all his Wheaties baseball cards for a bite.

It was after church camp we came to the river. This particular night, after the snapping turtle and before we went to our cots, Diane and I walked along the bank. The creamy mud oozed up between our toes. She said this was going to be the most important, most playing, turning-red-in-the-face summer ever, though this was the tail end of it. Her eyes were set dead ahead. Whatever she set out to do, she did, I knew.

That's the closest we got to talking about what happened in the tree; that and the badminton calamity were Diane's shames. Now, lying in my cot, watching the punched-out, pinpoint sky, I thought about two things: how pride goeth before a fall and how mine went forth and tripped me up last spring.

Right before school was out, the fourth and fifth grade girls challenged each other to a softball game. I was first one chosen for the fourth grade team because I was the best, and no one could deny it. I could hit a home run clear out of the school yard, farther than any boy; catch any flyball and scoop up any skinner even if I had to roll on the ground for it. But I was too proud to pick anyone myself, not even my friends, not even Pat Wheeler, the Methodist preacher's daughter and my sworn-in-blood friend, who was a good ball player, just not as good as you-know-who, and I had to think about the good of the team.

The day of the big game I could hear fifth graders saying, *watch out for that freckle-face in the blue shirt.* They meant me, and I felt so proud. I went to bat the first time and struck out. My second time, I barely hit the ball to shortstop. My third time at bat, the outfield, who at first moved out to the sidewalk when I came to bat, now sat down; the infield moved in. It got worse. When my team was in the field, I

missed every fly, every skinner. The fifth graders began to hit
their balls my way because they knew I'd miss them. We lost
the game because of wonderful me. I was never so mortified
in my life, not even when I was six and couldn't hold it any
longer and peed in church during the final prayer, in the front
pew.

Pat Wheeler forgave me, I felt so rotten, and things got
back the way they were before, with us playing tennis under
the arch of trees on Maple Street or going on bicycle expeditions up Buffalo Creek. But I knew now that what I'd learned
in Sunday School about pride was true, and I had better work
on being more humble and less puffed-up.

So this night on the river, we lay on our cots under the
stars. We could smell the clay of the river and hear it gurgling
around the willows that dipped their branches into it, and we
burned with our shames.

Maybe it's because we had them and didn't want them
that we learned two new words the next day: tenacity and
perserverance, and that we had them, too. What Diane did
was she caught that snapping turtle. She rigged up a fishing
pole, planted herself on that rock around where the turtle
lived and said she wouldn't come down till she had caught it.
That was morning. Later, in the heat of the day, Mother and
Daddy were lounging under the trees I was climbing in, and
we could see Diane still sitting out on that rock, not budging,
holding that line in the water. Mother had me take her a
sandwich, because Diane said if she left for lunch it might be
just when the turtle came.

In the afternoon I swam out to a place in the middle of
the river where a half-submerged tree caused swift eddies to
curl around it downstream. I resolved to start at the bottom of
the tree and swim upstream, against the current and through
the eddies, to the end of the tree and quiet water. I tried for an
hour, over and again, without stopping, straining against the
current that always pushed me downstream, but each time I

got stronger, got more practice. I pushed against the water one more time as hard as it pushed against me, then, with all my strength, gave an extra push, and, suddenly, I was past the place I could never get past before, upstream, past the swift eddies, in quiet water. I felt the sun and water on my face, and I felt strong and glisteny. Diane called to me, and I looked to see her dancing on the rock, swinging that snapping turtle from the end of her fishing pole. I waved from the water, and she yelled: *That turtle got me first, but I got it now!* Then she took it off the line and threw it back in the river. The sun was low in the sky and turning the river orange. We had hotdogs and chili beans for supper, and Mother and Daddy told us how they thought we both were something; how I had perservered, how Diane had snapping turtle tenacity. I could feel pride sneaking back up but thought, what the heck.

There was something special about that summer. We could sense it, as sure as the yellow grass, the crab apples and clay, as sure as the river and its business. But we couldn't pin it down.

A great thing happened the next afternoon. My family and I were taking our last walk through the woods and into the meadow, where we came across the First Methodist Church people from our town having a cook-out on Biggers Pond. Biggers Pond was more like a little lake far across as a football field. People of all ages, grown-ups down to kids my age, were about to have the Biggers Pond Great Race. All along the banks, they were getting ready to shove off in their rowboats, canoes, paddle boats and rafts.

Pat Wheeler shouted at me from a long rowboat full of kids. I felt mixed-up--happy for Pat and popping with envy. Oh, Diane and I wanted to race so bad, we were ready to change religions. How can you stand on the sidelines, watching those boats, and not go crazy for wanting to be part of it.

Daddy took Rev. Wheeler to the side and had a talk with him. Rev. Wheeler went over to some bushes dangling in the shallows and pointed out an old raft. It was green from moss and lopsided, and it was half-sunk in the lake from being waterlogged. The reeds that held it together were frayed and unraveling, but it was the only thing left. He said we could use it, why not let the Baptist preacher's girls join the Methodist Biggers Pond Boat Race?

We ran to the wonderful craft and shoved it into position down the bank. It was heavy as lead from water. I couldn't imagine how anybody could have let a good raft go bad like that when they could have been playing Pirates, or Finding the Northwest Passage.

It was time for the race. As Mother and Daddy walked away, I heard Mother say, *We might as well pitch a tent in the meadow and wait for the girls*; Daddy said, *Never mind, that wreck'll dissolve halfway across, and they can swim the rest of the way faster than the rowboats.*

Rev. Wheeler shot off his cap pistol, the landlubbers cheered, the racers shoved off, and I yelped, *Diane, where's our paddles? Oh, my gosh, paddles*, she said, searching all around. Stuck up under a bush were two planks, eaten up by bugs and crooked with drying wrong in the sun. We grabbed them and shoved off. The raft sank more into the water and lobbed from side to side, and Diane and I paddled mightily. *It's lopsiding, Diane,* I yelled. In a flash I was up in the air, hanging on to the side of the raft that went up. Diane was splashing underwater at the side that went down. I jumped in the water to save her, just as she came spluttering up to save me from being flipped to kingdom come. We dog paddled off and watched that raft flip all the way over. The underside was now topside, and it was even slimier with moss and water bugs. *At least,* said Diane, *we have more moss to hang onto.* She clenched hold of some. I did, too, and we started over.

All the boats out there smashed us with their wakes, even canoes. We could see the shore. Winners had already happened. Others were landing. Except the Jones girls, in the middle of Biggers Pond, on a dumb-looking raft going lop-sided. We who had gone unnoticed were being noticed. People on shore pointed and gawked. Reeds unraveled, and planks split off from the raft. Lake water sloshed up between gaps in the planks. What we did was, we folded it up with our legs like a sawhorse, we bent right to the water and paddled like crazy with our hands. All the time, the raft kept sinking deeper till it was all the way underwater. But all three of us-- the raft, Diane and me--kept going. All you could see were two girls laughing and sticking out of the water from the waist up, paddling like windmills and still sinking. Then it fell apart all the way. What was left of our sawhorse surfaced in pieces and went bobbing off here and there on the lake. Diane and I slipped into shallow water up to our necks and waded the rest of the way to shore. People who had been gawking clapped their hands. Mother smiled and shook her head, and Daddy beamed. Pat Wheeler hugged me and said she hoped we grew up to be sailors together. Diane and I shook hands. We did not win first prize, but Rev. Wheeler awarded us Mrs. Pogue's prize winning blueberry cobbler for our tenacity and perserverance.

Later that night, a bunch of us kids roasted marshmal-lows. They were perfect--burned black and crunchy outside, melting down the stick inside. The other kids all bragged like they had been on bedraggly rafts, too, instead of the regular, boring boats they'd really been on. I was pleased as punch, and proud, and if Sunday School didn't like it, it could go jump in a lake.

The next day was the day we left the river. It was a golden day but with a difference, a change in it; not fall, but a reminder of fall coming. Diane and I felt good. Now we and our friends would think of us at Biggers Pond, not at the everything-gone-wrong softball game, the awful badminton game. I asked Diane right out about the strange tree. She said there was nothing she could do about it and about what happened, but she was glad for Biggers Pond. *We made that old piece of trash turn shipshape, didn't we, Jane? Sure did, Diane.*

The last thing we did before we left was to swing on grapevines out over the river--that last summer before everything changed. Diane swung high and wide as ever, but she wouldn't be Tarzan anymore, so I couldn't be Boy or Gorilla.

I swung out over the brown water and wished I could hang there in space awhile before I had to swing back. I swung back to the bank and skidded up dust, just as Diane was hanging up her grapevine and saying she was going looking for more Biggers Ponds to jump in and get across. And she didn't mean real ones with real water. *Know what I mean?* she asked. I didn't know what she meant and just walked along, digging my toes through the dirt. *Hey, Diane,* I said, *want to chonk crab apples? No, I'm going up the river to do some thinking, for awhile. About what?* I asked. *Stuff you don't know about,* she said. *Can I come, too?* I asked. *No, go chase lightning bugs or something.*

Oh, okay, I said and watched her walk on ahead, all tall and slim. I felt kind of let down. I looked around for something appealing. All around, there were crannies, vines and lots of rotting crab apples. I picked one up and threw it hard as I could at an oak tree. It splatted just enough to satisfy.

Eloise Klein Healy

A Mile Out of Town
for my parents

The Golden Pheasant was the Travelleer,
was the Red Star before that,
was the place my mother tended bar
and managed the motel,
was the corner my dad owned
the garage and gas station.

One orange night lard caught fire
and burned the Red Star out of our lives,
burned the illegal punch boards
and the prizes hidden under the counter,
burned through grease soaked floors
and blacked all the hamburger buns stacked
in white cellophane boxes.

So we moved from the trailer
into the new motel and lived in the big unit,
the one next to the fuzzing neon sign
that flashed VACANCY or NO VACANCY
through the nights.
I learned to ride a bike there
in our front yard of red rock chips,
fishtailing and skidding with my mother
running alongside to steady the turns.

And we had a new place to work, the Travelleer.
Pine and sheet rock shingle siding and a red roof.

I told my mother goodnight there many times
behind the thick high bar, pushing my way
through grownups who hugged and gave me
whiskey kisses. There was always a half-breed dog
to follow me home.

Before I was in first grade I was tall enough
to look into the soapy dishwater,
could dry glasses and make them squeak,
could cut French Fries with my dad and lift
them in wire buckets out of the hot fat.
When we worked in the kitchen it meant Cook
was drunk, but he was a good cook and told me
stories, his cigarette sticking to his lip.
He had the only tattoo I'd ever seen and guessed
it must have come from the Navy.

The weekends were dance music and cars
turning in from the highway late at night,
people puking in the parking lot, men standing
by pickups talking and laughing with women,
June bugs in the summer frying themselves
on the neon.

We made beds and beds and beds
for accordion players, organ players
and sometimes a three piece band.

I mostly played alone,
was Gene Autry and Roy Rogers,
a football player in white sandals,
a paratrooper jumping off combines and cornpickers
with a Blo-Up life vest for a chute.
I begged my mother for guns and holsters,
rifles and footballs. She thought something was wrong

with me. I never pretended to be a girl
or wanted to dress that way.
I imagined skirts into fantasy ritual items
and wore hats to church as tribal garb.
Levis were all I wanted and I wore them
like a biker until the dye made my legs blue.

I hurried among adults, mumbling
like a radio left on low,
a running bedraggled pygmy in loose curls,
armed with sticks, old pans, a motley uniform
of pinafore top, brown oxfords, a red cowboy hat
and a coaster wagon, all of it beginning to be a poet,
talking to itself.

And every year on the feast of St. Nicholas
out of nowhere candy flew
through the window, the expected fruit of believing,
of being rooted there, growing up a mile from Remsen, Iowa
on the two lane highway
with the tall green corn all around.

Dreaming of Athena

A woman sits down
having listened to herself so long
she can no longer contain it,
and on clean paper
like a bird of final wisdom
sweeping sure out of the darkness
she begins to write:
I have always loved women,
so many women,

nests,
the complexities of branches,
birds rising in flight,
the owl who leaves no footprints,
the white egg in spring.
I wake up
and I'm different
as snow on dark ground,
snow feathered like a wing,
normal flight.
I wake up and it's different
out of the dream shell,
uncontained.

Anna Klein
for my grandmother

Anna Klein,
where are you in the husband and the children?

Your name drifts off into their stories
while you sat happy to get your hair pincurled
every Friday night during the boxing on TV.
Grandpa smoked the pipe and yelled
"god damn the bitch" when the boxers
wrestled instead of punched.

You were happy in the garden
and happy to be strong
and the first time you had time
to play with the children
you were the grandmother.

Why was I ashamed of you
in the cabbages and beets?
What was wrong to me with your vigor,
the length and repetition of labor?
You were a simple woman
who was found to like to write a letter.
And I was ashamed you kept your teeth
in a glass of water in the pantry.

Coming out

When Charlotte announced in the faculty room
that she had a romance in the summer and travelled
with him to places she was afraid to go
I thought of Mazatlan
and the first breath of air we took
as we got off the plane, the first
slam of tropical weather, not just
the literature or the drama,
but the heft of all the hot air
and then the baggage,
the sweating, the sleeping, the money,
the shrimp, the crosses, the dresses,
the silver.

I went to Mazatlan,
but more than romantic, I wanted to say.
I wanted to say just to be able to say
"my lover, you know, you met her.
We went to Mazatlan for five days
and I know what you mean
about being afraid.

Do you know what I mean?"

To Speak For Human Feelings

It's a dangerous feeling
to want to love and protect you
because I'll be human
that much longer.
I won't have to buy so many things
to be happy
and I'll be human that much more.

It's a dangerous gesture
to walk arm and arm with you
to the store
because I won't forget
where I came from—the need
for human touch,
and I'll be human
so much simpler
if it shows.

Every word I put on paper
is a shout against the distance
between us all,
and I'll be human
that much deeper
if my saying so
makes arms around your shoulders
and our silence come undone.

Eileen Pagan

EL TIEMPO PRESENTE
EN TODO MOMENTO

El tiempo presente en todo momento hoy me traslada ha
aquella amada isla a épocas que parecen tan remotas tray-
endo a la memoria a la nina juquetona e inquita llena de
incertidumbre en lo incógnito de su subconciencia.

Memorias...si el recuerdo, del recorido por los parques, el
caminar de su viejo y sus suenos muertos, el cancáncio de
la madre que en sus horas árduas buscaba el peso con que
comer.

Cuanta rabia al escuchar los cuentos de la abuela. A esta le
encantaba en especial contarle a la nina el de Caperucita
Roja. ¿Acaso no se daba cuenta ella que aquella historieta
ruborizaba de miedo a la pequena en todo su ser? A la nina
no le divertía saber que caperucita era una estúpida que no
se sabia defender. Pero bueno, hay un dicho que dice que
la ignorancia es atrevida.

En el barrio todas las senoras; Dona Pancha, Dona Ramonita, Dona Yeya, la abuela, se sentaban en el sillón, mece
que mece. Chismeaban de la hija de Dona Fulana, hablaban
de le novela de las once, el juego de pelota y como siempre
la política no podia faltar.

Todas de acuerdo estaban que aquella isla, Puerto Rico,
debia ser un estado libre asociado. ¡Qué disparate caray! y

Dios me libre que dijiera algo, porque, segun ellas, esta pila de mierda, en aquel entonces, no sabia nada.

Para la niña todo era vivir en armonía. Sin embargo, las dudas se presentaron con preguntas del proceder total y un sentimiento.

Ya mamá empezaba a preocuparse. Todos en el barrio comentaban de que rara era su niña. Decía la abuela que si esa marimacha no cambiaba veía a la pobrecita alla quemandose en el infierno.

Para la joven muchacha todo se convirtio en tormento. Sentimientos impuestos se hicieron presente...aquella amada isla comenzaba hacerse muy chica.

En un abrir y cerrar de ojos en busca de la llamada libertad se traslada la joven a un país extrano y frío...si, frío como la nieve.

En aquel infinito viaje rumbo ha lo desconocido, viajaba la *gran alcal5deza de San Juan* Doña Fela del Rincón con su gran moño, la gran señora. De repente el mónstro del avión, tiembló como si se fuera caer del cielo. Lo primero que vino a la mente de la joven muchacha fue que le llegó la hora a Fela y aqui se jodieron todos. Muy claro lo vió en el periódico en primera plana "Gran Trajedia! Muere Doña Fela del Rincón, la distinguida alcaldeza de San Juan, al estrellarse el avión donde viajaban 174 pasajeros. Todos Mueren." Y de joven muchacha nadie sabe nada...el mundo ni se entera de que existe....

Irónico, fué pensar, que aquel viaje tuviera la solución a su sentir. La lucha que comienza se hace interminable; cuanto que aprender; que infinidad de sorpresas: el obstáculo del

idioma; descubrir que es una "mujer de color," Latina,
Lesbiana. Nuevas aventuras, nuevas inquietudes, ais-
lamento y una soledad total....

Ademas, que desilución al encontrar que aún entre los
suyos existen prejuicios falsos. Lo intenta y se resiste y
otra vez intenta. El tiempo no se acaba y la historia apenas
comienza.

El deseo de vivír y crecér en cada instante.... Memorias
inovidables, vivas, que estan en su mente junto a una esper-
anza de vida a plenitud, confiando que el mañana no traera
envidias ni rencores.

En sus sueños, la hermosa melodía, el canto a la libertád,
un grito de solidaridád, estrechando fuerzas con voces
unánimes, debiles y fuertes, luchando sin prohibiciones.
En sus sueños, oye el canto tangible. En la realidád...cuan
lejano está.

TIME, EVER PRESENT

Time, ever present, today takes me to that beloved island,
to periods that seem so remote, bringing to memory the
playful and restless little girl filled with uncertainties in the
unknown of her subconscious.

Memories...yes, the recollection of the races through the
park, the walk of her old man and his now dead dreams...
the fatigue of her mother in her arduous search for the
dollar for food.

So much rage hearing her grandmother's stories. She loved
to tell that little girl the one about Little Red Riding Hood.

Didn't she realize that that tale flushed fear through the little one's entire being? The girl did not enjoy knowing that Little Red Riding Hood was so stupid that she could not even defend herself. Well, they say that ignorance is bold.

In the neighborhood all the wives, Dona Pancha, Dona Ramonita and Dona Yeya, the grandmother, would sit in their chairs, rocking and rocking, gossiping about Mrs. So and So's daughter, talking about the eleven o'clock soap opera, the ball game--and, as always, politics were not overlooked. All agreed that that island, Puerto Rico, should be a free associated state. "What damned nonsense!" they would say. The girl would not dare say a word, God forbid...she was, after all, a little shit who knew nothing of the world.

And yet, for her, the world was still full of possibilities of harmony. Soon, however, doubts would make themselves present. Soon, the ways of the real world would begin a gnawing sensation deep within her.

Mama began to worry. All the neighborhood commented on how strange her daughter was. Grandmother would say if that dyke doesn't change, she envisions that poor child burning in hell.

For the young woman, everything was converted into torment, the gnawing more intense. That beloved island became too small.

In the blink of an eye, a search for so-called liberty took the young woman to a land, foreign and cold, as cold as the snow.

On that eternal flight to the unknown, traveled the grand
mayor of San Juan, Dona Fela del Rincón, with her hair
grandly piled on her head.   She was a grand lady.   Suddenly, the plane began to tremble as if it were going to fall
from the sky, and the first thing that came to the young
woman's mind was that Dona Fela's time had come and
the rest of the passengers were fucked.   Very clearly she
envisioned the newspaper front page: "Grand tragedy!
Dona Fela del Rincón, the distinguished mayor of San
Juan, was in a plane crash with 174 other passengers.   All
dead!"   No one would know a thing about the young
woman.   The world wouldn't know she existed.

Ironically,   that voyage would bring a solution to her
feelings.   The unending struggle began.   So much to learn,
what infinity of surprises: the language barrier, discovering
she was a "woman of color," a Latina, a lesbian.   New
adventures, new restlessness, isolation and a total soli-
tude....

Consequently, what a disillusion to find that even among
your own there exist false prejudices.   She tries and resists
and tries again.   Time does not end, and history barely
begins.

The desire to live and grow at every instant....   Memories
that cannot be erased are lived in her mind with the hope of
a plentiful life, confident that tomorrow not bring envy or
resentment.

In her dreams a beautiful melody, the song to liberty, a
shout in solidarity, stretching with unanimous voices, both
weak and strong, struggling without inhibitions. In her
dreams, the song seems quite tangible. It is in reality that
the notes fade.

Gloria Ramos

Rush Hour Bunny

IT's GOOD FRIDAY, the friday before Easter, this guy gets on the subway rush hour carrying a huge pink plastic bunny, gets on, you know what I mean, he gets on at 14th Street, yeah, 14th Street, the uptown IRT subway and he is carrying this thing. This pink plastic bunny...and jeez it has to be four feet tall and he is carrying the damned thing in his arms like a baby. Sure it's close to Easter and sure some kid is going to be bug-eyed...but really on the subway during rush hour?

Do you know what the subway is...and specifically what it is during rush hour? The subway stinks, literally and figuratively. It's rows of connected metal boxes...cattle cars...stuffed full of people who ride by choice, habit, conditioning and necessity to and from work under the most appalling circumstances in civilized history. The subway has the odors of living and since it never gets scrubbed it has layer upon layer of smell pressed into its surface, and if you got a nose like mine, god love it, you can get a trace of something from one year ago! So this jerk, yeah, I am calling him a jerk, and an out-of-towner too, 'cause anybody who knows the city does not do something stupid like that! Like bring a plastic bunny on the subway! You need both your hands to stand upright, you need your strength just to hang on to those straps...oh the bunny's cute all right but the fuckin ears and feet are all over the place! And one of its paws is holding up this big carrot that keeps poking people's faces! So he is in, the doors squeeze shut and we are off again for 42nd Street.

The New York subway system is an underground network of interconnected tunnels. It's like a whole fuckin world down there, endless tunnels. There are maybe forty people crushed into a space where even twenty-five would fit tightly. But we have learned to squeeze and accommodate and give. The tapestry of smells. The urine stains on the walls. The vomit-splattered benches that no one wants to sit on. The winos and derelicts, the refuse of the city. In the subway there is no vegetation, there are no flowers or plants, there is no green, no air, no sunlight. There is nothing of nature in the subways except people. All else--concrete, steel, asphalt--all man- made.

The train lurches forward as we start the run to 42nd Street. The car is hot...it is always hot and stuffy...no fresh air gets into the subway system's air supply. It is cold outside in the mornings, so you dress for winter or early spring, but the subway is hot.

I am wearing a heavy coat and I have boots on. The air in the car is stale and heavy. One person is pressed against the other...you can smell what someone had for breakfast...you try not to smell the other person's breath but generally you are breathing what the other exhales. Everyone tries to keep cool. It is part of the system of existing in a big city, you have to learn to make room and this is often difficult. You want to yell, "get off my fuckin foot" or "give me some space" or "goddammit, I can't breathe." But you don't. You stare into space or at the ceiling. You don't do anything to draw attention to yourself, make waves or in any way show that you are not one of the participants in the game called BIG CITY.

The air is loaded with all manner of unsaid gripes as we all clutch the overhead straps and head home. The difference this time is that those bunny ears are sticking up over the people's heads. You gotta laugh, I think to myself, how you gonna get mad at a bunny?

The train slows down and comes to an abrupt stop that throws me off balance. There is swearing under breath as toes are stepped on. This is usual everyday stuff, however, so no one really reacts except to acknowledge it as a minor inconvenience, an annoyance. Everyday millions of bodies pour into the subway systems, surging through its maze of turnstiles and coin booths, flushing in and out of trains moving through the city like a giant sluice system, the subway's unnatural rivers. Everyday the cumbersome and depressing ritual continues --millions of people crushing into the subway each and every monday through friday of their lives, missed only on those saturdays and sundays off and during that wretched two-week vacation.

Though the silent riders try not to look at each other but through each other, or at a non-existent TV set in the ceiling, or outside at the black and ugly walls of the tunnel, they are standing in approximately the same square inch, and they are aware of each other. Because of the "over-utilization" of the subway system, it is often in disrepair and is neglected, which causes severe breakdowns in operations.

We have started and stopped a few times now. I am sweating. Jesus, this ride is slow. I wish there was some other way to get home. Maybe I could leave work early or later. I think the thoughts I have thought over and over without resolution. I have been sweating for ten minutes, sweat streaming down my face. I can't take off my coat or sweater, I do not have enough space! Wearing wool, the heat contained in my sweater threatens to blow up. I blow air from my lips down through my sweater, the air is hot and sticky and does no good. Underground in a dark dirty tunnel and boiling hot. The air is stale. I feel I will suffocate. All these people, jammed into them, ignoring me. I must stay cool, I know that all that's impinging on me will drive me mad. I must stay cool. I want to scream but don't, it isn't nice to make trouble. I look around the train and see the bunny, those bunny ears are sticking up. I look over at it for reassurance, but the bunny's plastic is picking up moisture, it is covered with a slimy-looking film, it looks like it's sweating.

I notice a woman, fifty-five or sixty, sweating profusely, who looks very, very nervous...something ominous about her eyes and face. I can see "it" in her eyes. "Don't scream," I whisper to myself, hoping that she will hear me or read my mind, but she does not. She does not see me. She is too busy looking at her own disaster pictures inside her head. "Don't scream." Her eyes go wilder with each pulse of her blood. Her glands are excreting the odor of fear. Others around her seem to pick up her scent. Excitement and anger are loose in the train car. Apprehension grips the people, who begin to speak out loud, daring to break the code that is inherently New York. "This is a pretty long time, isn't it?" "I've never know it to be so long." Now they've done it--verbalized the silent fear of every passenger. An hour, not moving, stuck underground for one hour. In this heat, in this crowding. The reality of the moment grips me. Don't scream anyone, I won't be able to stand it, I'll go crazy. I've got to get out of here. I look around. I am trapped on this train with these people. The woman is white. She is still in an eerie way. I look for the bunny, trying to distract myself, but what I see makes me more frightened. The guy holding the bunny is sweating, the sweat rolling down his face, and he cannot wipe it because of the bunny he is holding. The bunny is slimy and sticky, giving off an odor, a sickening odor. I am smelling all kinds of strange things...dust, filth, perspiration...and...smoke...oh my god, I am smelling smoke. I put my hand over my mouth...FIRE...I was going to yell, FIRE, oh my god. My nose is intent on "seeing" what I cannot see. The fans stop. Stillness. There is deadly silence. The fans at least gave us a sense of motion, movement now with their cessation we are suspended in time, no sound, no action. We look at each other, unspoken questions fly about us: what is happening? are we going to go again? why don't they move this train? Then the lights go out. My blood stops running, fight or flight instincts leap into alert.

The lights flick back on again. A wave of relief and light-headed laughter sweeps through the train.... "Wow," someone exclaims, "that was scary."

Someone reaches over and slaps the bunny ears playfully and everyone nearby smiles as the train lurches forward and starts to move again. A few moments later we enter 42nd Street. Grand Central station and there are hundreds of people waiting for the train and no one gets off. The memory of events of a few short seconds ago fades quickly as I compliment myself on my good fortune of already being on the train and pride myself for not being one of those who either has to wait for another train or force and push my way onto this one. Hordes of people are trying to get on the train that we smugly occupy. When the hardy ten or twenty souls who have the energy and stamina push, shove, edge, grab and somehow squeeze in to where it was not humanly possible, the doors close and we are off again to 86th Street, which is the next stop. It's the one where I get off and change to the Queensboro line for the final leg of my daily journey home.

The train moves out of the station but does not completely clear it. It stops half on, half off the station.

I look over at the guy with the bunny and he is smashed up against the door at the end of the train. I can't see him, but I can see the huge ears sticking up and a bit of the bunny's carrot above the other heads.

The train is at a dead stop in the tunnel. I look through the filthy window and wonder what is out there. It must be dirty and dark. Crocodiles. I remember stories about crocodiles in the subway system. What a thought. "Stop it," I say to

myself. Shivers run through me. I am fascinated by the
thought and it keeps entering my brain more insistently
because of the energy I am using to try and stop it. If I had to
crawl through the tunnel I wouldn't be able to make it without
screaming. Breaking into tears. What would happen to the
bunny? Hey, where is the bunny?

We have again been stopped for a long time. The fans
stop. The lights start flashing and blinking on and off. Mut-
ters of "piss" and "shit" punctuate the air and are strangely
reminiscent of thunder from a far away storm. The middle-
aged woman starts sweating profusely again and her eyes
have that eerie look. People are beginning to mutter. Silent
prayers are sounded as "Hail Mary's" break cover and reach
for the open air. The smell of fear is in the train car, stronger
than before. "What the hell is going on?" shouts an irate
taxpayer, reaching his endurance. He drones on about the
breakdown of the subway system and how this will lead to
the eventual breakdown of civilization as we know it. Few
are listening.

A strange thing is beginning to happen. I can't explain it,
but people are squeezing toward the doors and windows, as if
trying to get out. Struggling to evaporate through the windows and into the air outside...struggling to become air and
disappear out of the tunnel and up towards the tall buildings.

I see a light outside. A flashlight. A rumble goes through
the car. No, I think to myself, don't scream anybody. Don't
scream FIRE or anything. Be calm. I want to say it out loud
but I can't. It gets really tight on the train. The air is getting
hot, electric, people are trying to look out of the windows and
see what is going on outside. And then she screams. That old
lady I had been watching, lets out this horrifying *we are
trapped, and this time we are going to be buried alive* scream
that instantly communicates to everyone and sets in motion
every sick statement that has been said for centuries about
crowds, tunnels, fear and most of all, panic.

At the other end of the train a tidal wave begins, rises and swells toward the exit door on my end of the train. People crowding and pushing with nowhere to go because the doors are closed and no one has enough room or space to open them. Yelling, "take it easy," "someone fell," screams and shouts fill the air. Back and forth from one end of the train to the other the human wave moves, pummeling everything in its way, trying to find a shore. The solid mass moves from one end to another each time leaving some damage, some refuse, pressed against the car walls. I'm scared. God I am scared. I can feel the urine involuntarily leave my bladder and begin to trickle down my legs and the trickle becomes a river that I am powerless to control. I grab hold, the wall, the strap, a window, anything. I try to become paper thin. I want to be invisible. Something is wrong; please open the doors.... The words bounce off the car walls and disappear unheard and unspoken. My throat is dry and my eyeballs feel as if they will press my eyes out of the sockets and fall into the crowd and be trampled. Trampled, my god someone is being trampled. I am pulled by some magnetic, centrifugal force beyond my control into the wave moving from one end to another. I become aware of walking on something, on some-one. The thought almost makes me stagger. People are pushing very hard now, trying to force the walls of the train outward, trying to make space, make exits. I wish I could see the bunny. There is a voice and it is connected to a flashlight outside of the train and it is saying, "Breakdown ahead, no need for alarm, have you out in a few seconds." But it is too late. What is gripping me and the others is a savage urge to survive, to keep standing and moving with the wave, to stay upright. If I stop, I know I too shall fall. Shall fall and be swept away and under. I must keep moving though it means walking on faces, arms, legs and hearts. I must keep moving if I am to survive.

The whistles and shouts from the outside try to stop what is happening inside, but it is useless. We are caught. We are screaming and moaning for things we never had. We are crying for ourselves, we are thinking of ourselves. We are pushing and screaming and I am an integral part of the whole. We are molded together, we are pressed as one into a will and determination that we have no control over and are powerless to oppose. I am pushing and walking on my fellow men, women and children, and it is all right.

A door opens on the far end of the train, a flashlight attracts the attention of the indiscriminately violent wave and it turns and hurls itself toward the beam of light outside the open exit.

In the glare of flashlights I can see, in a corner of the car, what was once a man and his proud possession . The deflated pile of teeth and clothing, bunny ears and blood, were crushed in a collage, forever together, inseparable.

The wave stumbles toward the door. In seconds it is out and still, quelled, dissipated. A silence fills the tunnel. I am out and suddenly a tremendous sense of guilt grips me. We the now individual drops of the mighty wave cannot look at each other. Although the tunnel is dark and we cannot see each other, we each know what the other is thinking. We are glad to be alive!

Jacqueline de Angelis

No Matter What I See from This View
No Matter How Long I Look and Look Again
the Situation Is the Same

SUN BLANK AND YELLOWING on the beige columns of stucco. Cars and cars in military rows, a sane, a comfortable distance apart. Just like myself from my friends. Just like myself from myself. Or, not like myself at all.

I bleed onto the freeway going south. 55 or 65 or 85 it doesn't matter, what matters is that I am moving. The curves in the road become my spine twisting to accommodate: my left side to the cement divider, my right to the cars approaching from behind. The City of Commerce, although prosperous, hides itself in a chain link dress and hangs over itself a dull, working sky.

Back at work I wad papers, write memos to file about my tour of the Smith Tool Company. So that someone will feel justified, I figure and refigure my budget. It is the depression, I say to someone in the bathroom who hopes I have a nice day. Who, the next day, passes me an article on Jesus under the divider between the stalls. I don't need hope. Simply to listen to myself like one would listen to the radio.

Last night it was the faucet. Butter nut butter nut butter nut, I translated the water for hours. Over and over it fell onto the stainless stopper. I am going to fix it one of these days, but last night I was planning its demise the way it planned mine over and over with the regularity of butter nut. I was judging myself systematic and predictable, unlike water not flexible enough to do a pretzel with my body or my emotions, as I turned over in bed and was reminded of my mother pointing to her leaking swimming pool. It was incomplete without the lap of waves reacting to a diver. Give in to the wave, I heard my dead father say. Give in to the wave and you won't be hurt, be drowned. I fought the waves until the day I decided to run body first, head turned around to watch my father watching me run into it fearless. Tossed, I dove into it, came up on the other side firmer in the water.

It isn't really a view. Not something I'd write about in my journal, nor would I speak of it in passing as the lovely, the interesting, or even the view from my office window. It offers an unadorned look into the hospital employee parking lot and, further to the west, the side of the hospital. Up at the top, the sky is a sliding rectangle. Below, seen when my face is to the glass, a torn piece of paper near a vent on the tar roof flutters endlessly. I know the Chevies, the Mercedes, the vans, and Hondas, but rarely see the owners, or see them shaded in the structure carrying their lunch bags, brief or hospital cases. This parking structure levels the classes.

At work I hear the news of the sun and moon pulling at each other like no other time in history. I am not surprised, nor do I count on it to explain my current situation. So what, I say to the astrologist. But not only that, she tells me, it's cosmic because something and something are in something. And yes, times are rotten, and I agree it hasn't been a time to recommend being born. I open the door to our house thinking of St. Helen's volcano and the contaminated Love Canal. No one is home, so I am left alone to drink sherry, to stare out the window, to see again the web that has been there for six months.

It appeared during the middle of December. Before Christmas. On Christmas it swung in the draft, became full and two-dimensional in the smoke from the joint I was smoking. The house was cold and so were my resolutions, my feet, and my coffee when I stepped out of the shower. I went out on the back porch where it was colder, and the eucalyptus leaves swung on the trees like baby machetes. And out on the porch I ran into another web that curled around my little finger, moist, momentarily elastic, and slippery like sex between my fingers. But I couldn't get out. Like the fly, like the ant, the occasional bee, the beetle, the ordinary grub, I was caught and it followed me to the holiday dinner, through my drive back to L.A., to the house cold, and the web turning in the moonlight above the window frame.

That night I dreamed of our legs toward the end of the bed linked and familiar. But when I woke to the TV light I was alone, wandering across the bed with my hand over the distance that was more than miles or time.

I got up and turned the grey matter off the set. I got up for milk, sat in the metal chair rocking to the overcast westside of L.A. It was too dramatic a view for me, so I opened the back porch door without creaking to find the trees simulating rushing water, the sky dark with the darker outline of palms and pine on it. I wanted to lie in the arms of her undivided attention and couldn't.

History has a way of repeating itself, I said at work. The 80's don't seem to me to know exactly what to repeat, so they begin by running all shows at once. There is the depression, surrounded by the beginning stink of war, and renewed cour-

age. The TV blares red, white, and blue. The radio, the
fifties. And the present roots of religion seem to be grabbing
the passing feet of my family members and those I work with.
Even the future's dragged in by corporate promises.

At work I'm given the tools of performance evaluation
and budgetary restraint. At home the water slaps against the
walls for me deeper than I expect. My momentum is broken.
Go on go on go on, I tell myself, go on without the need for
anyone's acknowledgment. Go on go on the bus down Sunset, go on go on walking up the hill. Everything I touch
circles about me, even a gift I've been given suddenly
shatters and I try to put aside the symbol.

At work they celebrate an opening and toast, behind his
back, one that is leaving, calling him a loser. He clears his
office out, leaving the wastebasket on the desk—a symbol
others by the coffee machine try to decipher. Caught in his
gesture for days, they will squirm nervously. I have no
opinion. From what I can see it was his only inexplicable
move.

At home construction becomes a metaphor. St. Helen's
explodes again. I turn around and turn around in my trust. I
hope that my memories will shore me. The blur of my life
tumbles me into my office. It's July, and the stucco's bright
in the flat sun.

LUNCH
#3

WHEN RAY DAVENPORT hit the pole in the parking garage,
Gina had the familiar feeling that this was not the way to
begin the day. The courier may have seen Gina and then

scurried into the elevator or he may have not.

But there she stood while the elevator vacationed on the sixth floor. Bonnie didn't make it in on time. Yuki came to her office in tears—she was sick of being a machine. All this before Gina's first cup of coffee must have distracted her from the car alarm in the parking structure that posed as the view from her office window.

"Give it to Gina, she will know how to handle this," she heard Bernie say as she came back from the coffee machine.

"Give me what, Bernie," Gina said, fingering the rim of the hot coffee cup.

"Gina, look at you, purple is your color, honey. Look, Gina, let's have lunch on Thursday. Right now I've got to run." Bernie slipped the memo into Gina's hand and grabbed Ralph by the arm.

Gina frequently forgot how important it was to have reflexes. Damn good reflexes she told Marina. But Marina had too many things to do to listen to Gina's babble.

"Sure," Marina automatically responded.

Gina closed her door but there was no escaping the sound of the persistent car alarm. She called security. Victor wanted to know the license plate number on the car. There was no way to convince Victor that she had no idea which of the hundreds of cars in the structure was making the sound, only that she heard it and knew it was coming from level four.

"I can't help you with such little information to go on," Victor insisted. Victor was a busy man, why, this morning he escorted a bum from the Sunset Boulevard entrance, he opened the locked Xerox room on the third floor, and he took a report on a stolen purse from a woman in the word processing center. He was busy, too busy to chase after a car she couldn't even identify. Victor was sorry.

Mr. Sanders called Gina. He didn't want it like that. He was taking it to the head of Planning, Research, and Develop-

ment. Nurse Practioner, Ann DiMargio, called and just
wanted to give Gina the message that her boss would not
accept the cover design. Her boss wanted Gina to send it back
and he would take it to the head of hospital administration.

Danny told Laura that Peggy Lee was taking an hour
lunch on a consistent basis and Laura was telling Gina.
Peggy Ann wanted to know if Gina could run over and look at
the sketch that had to go out in an hour. Bob Summerfield
came by to remind her about the report that was due.

By the time she opened her mail Gina was contemplating
the damage that could be done with a simple artist's X-Acto
knife. Perhaps it was even possible to kill with an X-Acto
knife. It was only 11:45 a.m. but Gina already saw the karma
of this day.

At lunch her cat vomited a hair ball on the sketch she
worked on during the weekend. She smiled while her mind
figured the line between murder and calm. She came home to
feed the grey cat and then returned to a meeting of adults who
fingered paper clips, chewed on their lips, or smoked and
smoked and smoked and smoked their guts out.

The alarm continued until 2:30 p.m. when it began to
dim like headlights left on in the rain.

M'Lissa Mayo

clear vigilance   black   with green
   glassy
   bright
   yellow   crystalline
never to be tainted by thoughts obscene
   perfection
needing leaves and needles jabbing
   at truth stabbing
a caring voice tells me never tell the leader
   if the leader is living on earth
even if the leader is living on earth
               part time

i bash my brain if i tell the teacher the truth
i bash my brain with the teacher's only hand

i simply covet silence

clear vigilance   black   with green
glassy
   bright
      yellow   crystalline
never to be tainted by thoughts obscene
       perfection

GREENSLEEVES..........POLLYTRIGGER
river clenched in a fist
            flowing through all
            four ehehehexhisting fingers
            on a set of potentially large
                    crane clatches
HEY YOU HEY YOU HEY YOU
                            across the parking lot
                        into transport mode, i died
                i
                    i
                        i
            i died, but only a bit, i died
I STILL SAW THE WORLD
    AND IT'S INNOCENCE
BUT THE INTELLECT
                    from another place
angrily, had me for a guest
TWO BEAUTIFUL WOMEN   SIT   IN AN ALMOST
BEAUTIFUL ROOM
        thinking painfully beautiful thoughts they say
            I FEEL   I FEEL   I FEEL
        they say separately to individual therapists

TWO LADIES IN A NOT SO PRETTY HOUSE
                                    PLUMBING POOR
    WE FEEL   WE FEEL   WE FEEL
                                    TOURIST VISION
        oddly,
            eyes glued to permanent beauty
            glassy reflection

IMPERFECT PYRAMIDS

WE STRIVE TO PERFECTION
    STUMBLING FALL
     WE TOPPLE
     WE JAM
       but oh how we can imperfectly improvise
        lopsided
                        axisymmetrically
                                  funny huh..
           how the broken glass usually shatters
                                in triangles...

            BAREFOOT

          BLEEDING   SHOD
          IN GRINDING
            shrinking
             sneeze
          opaque powder
             TO

         BENDING POINT

Ruchele ZeOeh

Sing Me Rich

Sing me.
Wing me some.
Sing me more vibes
from stretched sounds
vibrating soft to reach me full,
touch me loud, oo-oo sounds, ummm, woud, wowed.

Subtle-tease,
you are tren-chant.
Here, I hear you GO in your
U-kneek-U-bick-don't-quit-us now
slow stride riding oh so prrr-oud
uncrowded in your steamy-dream-world.
Never no-thing, never non-ness, always some
thing tingles me rare, cerebral to sing with loose
quavers, tight pulse, crisp ar-tic-U-elated, so-lo.

Bounce bountiful, gutsy
clusters grrr-off me again,
anytime your word-frames form
vibrations in sync, climbing on
too, into timed, far-out sonic clicks.
Sonorous, resonant, multisonant plosives,
d-d-s, t-t-s, that amuse in non-cleated time
becoming uncloned; becoming round-pound-multi-sounds.

Rich you are.
Rich to give more.
Gut sense is yours
always more sens-U-ous.

Clad olive-khaki, shod yellow,
you are dapper, mellow, cadence-caressive
honey. Ding your dogged-dongs-anytime-again-when?

Sing me.
Wing me some.
Sing me some, more Rich.

Cycling Classy

Hell-bent for
hot-rod heaven,
your turbo sails
unsignal'd lane change.

You zip,
tail,
swerve close,
unsettle my steerage.

Should I
unclutter
your headway
action?

You tandem
trunk in,
flank your tank,
swipe my bumper.
I concede
a connect.

A classy mass
blast-buster;
we clip
ride head-long
fast on our tails.

Star-Vexed Billie

Born too early
gone too soon.
Tragic girl
long gone
much too soon.
Put down fast
jostling for
freedom,
pushed around for
telling it like it is
defiant with her truth.

Moving down to bleak bistros,
sashaying up to
hoitytoity Cafe Society,
Billie's on-stage ease and
smooth-phrase cadence
stirred soothe-velvet from
Tin Pan Alley trivia
celebrating pleasure,
lamenting "Strange Fruit,"
concealing her
misery-clad sadness.

Gardenia doll trusted
users, bruisers

who left miseries
her middle name.
Quivered lips
cried bitter
rivers unstaunched
by fancy threads,
furs, limousines,
pretend happiness.
Baltimore oriole's
night wails ripped
spangled dreams,
shafted dawn's renewal.

Fifteen years beat, busted dol-drums,
torments mean-scene, jazz-daze, drug-craze
junkied uptight to oblivion
by heartless cruiser-losers.
God blessed this child,
jinxed her out-of-sight
behind bars. For what?

Ty-rant bureau-crazies
banned Billie's honey mode
from Big Apple digs.
Govern-mental clowns hounded.
Petty bureauc-rats shackled.
Billie foundered,
helpless, horizontal,
unraveling down
her alone-some-road.
Tortured gliss-glides,
shaky intonations mocked,
magic Holiday touch gone,
Disbelievers deserted,
no compassion for

heavy traveling,
loss of a frail'd spirit.
Listen closely
to wax tokens:
melodic cascades
bittersweetened
weary beyond belief.
Peer jazz luminaries shone as
Billie's star-vexed blaze dimmed,
skimmed the horizon
slowly going, gone.

She told us,
"Ain't none of your business what I do."
We said,
"Lady Day, it was everybody's business
what was done to undone you."
Born too early, fated to be gone,
long gone too soon.

Jeri Castronova

LAST LEGS

O Father Zeus — I see your heavy hand extending
out to reach into all forms of self-expression.
    Your patriarchal influence abounds in all we do,
    all we say and feel
    so that our women's hearts are all but closed
    to their true feminine power.
    We react as we were taught —
    making nice
    being pretty
    and not getting angry —
    not as powerful creative creatures
    which we are, whose inner cores
    run deep and passionate and
    opposite to the delicate, dependent
    and docile beings we've become.

Tell me, Zeus, why does the stiff demanding voice
of your commands so deride your daughters' freedoms?

    Why must the adulation you require be tempered with
    the need to swallow up the ones who go their own
    way?

    Your legacy I fear has seen too much sunlight
    through the centuries while cursing out the
    darkness.
    Our men refrain from nodding to the Goddesses

and stomp their likenesses into the ground.
They take the once-proud glory of the oracles
and proclaim their divine utterances as their own —
Apollo stands today as the sun god
while he it was who ursurped and raped
the divine oracle at Delphi and took her power.

O Zeus, hear your daughter's plea to restore the
rightful place in the pantheon to those works are
no longer kown — those Goddesses who lived so long ago
and live for us today as qualities of life.

The Magic Feather

She swings above applauding crowds
with deafened ears
above ordinary sets whose dancing bears
and jaded clowns and pawing ponies
perform their paces over and over again
to shrilly unrehearsed tunes
that fall on ears grown numb through years
to sameness and neglect
while she in savage innocence
swings high into the sky
and catches the magic feather
dropped from the mythic eagle-star
who dips a wing as it departs
to show its majesty
and then proclaims that only once
does such a bird bestow
the gift of its own cloak .
And through the centuries
those who win

the jet black feather soar the highest
of all their species—
whether human, fowl or mammal—
and when adversity of grieving times
sets in to leaden down the heart,
reach out the feather with an
outstretched arm into the bird's domain
and call it back to earth
where eagle-toned its words would fly
to that which caused despair.
With a stroke
it would smooth the road once more.

She sails above the crowd
afloat in hallowed space
into the arms of he
who never fails to catch his love
nor slows the rhythm of his swing.

One night the graceful artist flew
into her lover's grasp
and back again
but missed his catch
and so she fell...
she saw herself descend
as one who watches years
of wayward life go by and
cannot yet protest
the colored streaks of blurred
mosaic memories
an accompaniment to the quick reversal,
then the net—
caught
safe

trapped.
The net that breaks the fall
teases death and traps the victim
in its web.

Loose and rolling,
she lay amid the rumpled fold
of netting
looking up
and longing up
and watching down
at all the scurrying crew,
dancing donkeys
and padded clowns that said:
Hey, we're here too—
you two can't fly forever—
come down to where we are.

She flipped onto the
sawdust ground and strolled
among the bears, elephants and
twirling plates,
the running bareback riders
competing, all, for crowd-eyes,
with the tightrope walkers
and jugglers.

She breathed pungency of mustard
mixed with popcorn, sweat
and leavings of horses;
now and then a breeze
would blow sweet fragrance
of cotton candy and plastic stars
and candy apples.

She heard, all together, clatter
of clown's buggies and fire engines,
howl of talking dogs
and hurried tempo of the rasping band
and the joyous cheers and shouts
of the crowd.

She looked around at how
a stultifying mass remains among the glitter,
color and overstimulation
of the senses,
until despair set in
to remind her of
the price of safety.
She felt the sorrow of the heavy past,
she saw the pit within which
she once had lived,
the gravel rocks she carried
from the quarry to the stonewall,
never-ending,
where mere words were crushed
beneath her slavish steps
her heart so atrophied in time
it labored just to beat.

She felt the feather in her hand—
the jet black gift of eagle-star—
and felt its tugging to return
to glimpses rarified.

She knew
oh yes, now knew
the only time she felt alive
was when she really flew.

Fast climbing to the top-most ledge,
released now from the net below,
she got her flying feet
and soared into her lover's hands,

while slowly overhead
the eagle-star flew.
Attendant on its great ascent
it spiraled
to catch a melting sky.

Ashley Black

Walking Through Fire
a novel excerpt

WALKING THROUGH FIRE is a novel about a love triangle and about obsession. The points of this rather unique triangle are a 43-year-old mother, who is a colonel in the U.S. Marines, Glynnis Nikos; her 19-year old daughter, Angela; and the daughter's 24-year old married friend, Thea Patrikus, a graduate student from Greece. Glynnis and Thea have an affair of obsession, marked by a ravenous sexuality. The first excerpt describes Glynnis and Thea on the night they tentatively begin their affair. The second excerpt describes them and their passionate affair three months later.

THEA WAS THE LAST ONE off the plane. She ambled through the crowd, pretending not to look for Glynnis. An untied shoelace flapped awkwardly around her ankle.

Scolding herself for the impulsiveness, but out of control, Glynnis rushed toward her, excusing herself through the crowd. She stopped six inches in front of Thea, her hands with a mind of their own, extending toward the young woman, but at the last minute, she transformed the gesture into something casual that fooled neither of them, ran the left hand nervously through her hair and reached for Thea's carry-on bag with the right.

They didn't speak; they nodded and Glynnis kept the corners of her mouth from forming a smile, but she couldn't stop her eyes. Thea looked away and asked, "Where's the car?" as she walked on past Glynnis.

In the car Glynnis looked at Thea and took a plunge.

"It's late. Perhaps we should give ourselves a day in New York before going back."

"That sounds great," Thea responded before the sentence was out of Glynnis' mouth.

They checked into a hotel on Central Park West. Glynnis requested a room with two beds, as Thea pretended not to hear.

Concealing their mutual excitement, they rushed into the elevator and up to the eleventh floor, but once in the room, nervousness took over completely.

Thea tested and commented on the firmness of her bed. Glynnis tested her own in turn and found it to be sufficiently firm also.

"I haven't been to New York in over a year," offered Glynnis.

"Longer for me," offered Thea.

"It's great to have this chance."

"It is."

But both women were reluctant to suggest anything that would take them out of the room in which they were so uneasy.

"Perhaps..."

"Yes?" Thea was eager.

"A walk through the park."

Thea stood. "That's best. A walk through the park."

Glynnis stood, and they both moved for the door at once.

"Sorry," said Glynnis, as she jostled Thea. She stepped aside to let Thea through the door first.

"I have the key," Glynnis said.

"Good."

They sauntered along through Central Park, sometimes leaving the paths to cross to another part. After the long chafing days of winter, they could feel the first palpitations of spring, like the wings of butterflies fluttering to unwrap themselves. The ground, saturated from melted snow, was a lemon-mauve, and its muddy cover was starred by spots of bright green grass.

When they left the path, last year's fallen leaves, gray and sooty, squished into the moist earth. Glynnis found the sound of the leaves and Thea's rapid voice comforting, and she walked along, silent and relaxed. A piece of her that had been removed was back in place.

"Dennis has been pressuring my parents," Thea said with irritability. "They want me to marry now. Forget school. Be a good Greek Wife. Stuff grape leaves, pickle olives, and make baklava and babies."

"They can't force you. They can't take away your scholarship." Glynnis spoke slowly to control her voice.

"They can speak to the Greek consulate and make it difficult for me."

"Aren't they proud that you're a student?"

Thea shook her head. "They say what good is a doctorate in Classics. It won't help me raise sheep or children."

Glynnis touched Thea's shoulder in a comforting, almost maternal way, and Thea managed to take the tenderness without complaint.

They walked past the skaters' pond, empty and dirty now. Glynnis paused to watch the mallards padding in the yellowish pool, then looked at Thea as she turned round to wait for her.

Thea looked toward Glynnis, squinting and smiling into the frail sunlight, and Glynnis knew then that she wanted this woman. Wanted her with a recklessness she had never experienced. In a way that frightened her. She had lost her innocence.

She thought of those stories of Marines on Iwo Jima, charging into the face of flame throwers to reach their destination. She had always found that image stupid; she still did.

Thea took her hand and they left the pond.

They went to dinner and a nightclub, stayed out late, afraid to go back to the hotel room, just as they were anxious for the privacy.

In the nightclub, Thea was irritable and impatient. Glynnis watched the violent puffs of smoke and the eyes that would not look at her.

"What's upsetting you?" she asked Thea. "Thinking about your family still?" But she knew with certainty that Thea wasn't thinking about her family at all.

Thea looked at Glynnis. "What kind of relationship do we have anyway?" She said it as though she had a right to expect something, as though Glynnis had been leading her on.

Glynnis' eyes met Thea with the special middle-aged calm that she usually reserved for dealing with brash lieutenants. "We're friends."

Thea shifted angrily and lit another Gitanes. "There's more."

Glynnis shook her head slowly.

Thea persisted. "There could be."

Glynnis found herself being honest, learning something about herself in the process.

"I'm forty-three. If I throw myself into a passionate love affair now, at this time in my life..." She shrugged and looked away.

"It's frightening. If it works out badly, I don't know... One doesn't get a lot of second chances at my age."

Thea settled back in her chair, relaxed and cocky, and finished her drink. She had what she wanted.

If it all began at this point, Glynnis could remember no more of the context, but she remembered the rapid, troubled voice saying something like: "And if it should happen to us. What would you feel?"

Before Glynnis could answer, Thea turned to a passing waiter, not their own, and asked for the check.

Glynnis said, "It must not happen to us."

Thea looked back across the table, with an unstable laugh. "But let us suppose," she insisted.

Glynnis replied carefully, the mania for self-justification seizing her. "I wouldn't mistake it for self-indulgence. Simply, we have something to learn from each other."

In the hotel room, the maid had already turned down the beds, and the sight of the white sheets, bared and ready for them, frightened them both into shyness, even as it excited them.

Glynnis called room service and ordered drinks and a Greek salad.

With only the reading light on Glynnis' headboard to illuminate their clandestine conversation, they sat together on Glynnis' bed, picking at the salad, and spoke of the drive back. Glynnis' pass was only through the next day. Glynnis suggested that Thea must be tired from the long flight and the long day.

Taking in the warm gold of Glynnis' hair and skin honeyed almost to the tone of burnt sugar by sea-bathing in the Caribbean, Thea rapidly denied any fatigue, but supposed that Glynnis was tired, and made an insincere motion to rise and cross the small rectangle of padded carpet that separated the two beds.

Concealing the jump of panic in her heart, Glynnis emphatically asserted that she rarely needed more than four hours of sleep, and spontaneously grasped Thea's wrist.

Thea smiled crookedly, took a deep breath, and ran a hand through Glynnis' fine hair.

That was all it took.

Glynnis leaned across the starched bed sheets and placed her lips on the back of Thea's neck precisely where the neck curved into the shoulder blades. She had known the skin would be soft, but the shock of that neck--warm, smooth, and supple--sent a hot current through her torso, and she embel-

lished the kiss with touches of her curling tongue and finally
with a series of nibbles.

Thea turned her face to Glynnis' and kissed her, deri-
sively it seemed, antagonistically, on the mouth.

"We have something to learn from each other," Thea said,
her kisses soft, breathless stabs punctuating her words.

Glynnis tried to interrupt with some sort of well-formu-
lated reproach, but only managed to ask: "Is this the way?"

Thea didn't respond but pressed herself upon Glynnis like
someone pressing upon a bruise, then rolled over and pulled
Glynnis atop herself. In the fragile quivering context of every
kiss Glynnis found a brief respite from pain. When Glynnis
slid her hand under Thea's shirt and brushed the warm
smooth skin of her breast, it came with a relief, like ice on a
throbbing hangover, and Thea bit down on Glynnis' lip.

In that long night, Glynnis recognized Thea as a true child
of the Levant, whose women are fated to be the voluptuaries
not of pleasure, but of a painful obsession, doomed to seek
what they least dare to find.

At dawn their bodies roused them to carnal indulgence,
rapacious to a point approaching gluttony. Between those
breathless half-seconds when Glynnis felt the moistness of
that soft mouth on her lips and those long slender limbs
closing upon her own, spots of white light, like white noise,
shot like diamond bullets through her brain.

They rose and dressed quickly, disinclined to shower,
packed, and left the hotel. Not a word spoken.

● ● ● ● ● ● ● ●

They took the train to Boston, barely able to remain respectable during the trip, and rushed into the women's toilet
compartment together as the train rushed up the Connecticut
coastline.

In Boston they took the historical walk through cobble streets of the old town, and they stopped inside a frame church built in 1723. An Episcopal bishop was performing a service, and devotees were scattered about the front and middle of the church. The back was empty.

Glynnis inspected a heavy iron gate that separated the baptistry from the rest of the church. It opened, and she entered. Thea followed and closed the gate behind them.

Sunlight filtered through stained-glass windows into the prison-like baptistry, and bars of the wrought-iron gate cast long shadows across their faces and limbs. Glynnis pushed Thea into the shadows on the wall, and they kissed.

The bishop's voice could be heard reciting, histrionically, the Lord's Prayer. The choir sang Bach. With the chanting and singing and the vibrations of the organ, shrouding the other world, Thea unbuttoned Glynnis' blouse and jeans. She made love to her on the floor of that 200 year old church. At one point, she placed her hand over Glynnis' mouth to prevent her from being heard.

They left the baptistry separately, Glynnis first. Thea dipped a Kleenex in holy water, sponged her face and followed quickly, leaving the gate ajar.

They joined arms outside and hurried, giggling, down the venerable wooden steps.

minns

Secret

"Dust is the only secret..."
— Emily Dickinson

I've heard them,
poets,
sometimes the priest, but
it's not
the truth.
In the night
the stars
moving through the thick damp
up from the sea,
their scent so close to women
it speaks our name,
the stars
rolling around each other
through that excellent dark
know more than dust, know
more than we will
ever see but
have no names for it.

In the marsh
the peepers lament,
crying to each other
crying themselves to sleep
deep
in the long bones of bamboo
that mark

the edge
of the salt creek.
They know more than dust.

Their language
one of dybbuk and dinosaur,
they are the
godchildren
of spells,
a step towards them
means silence
quiet
cut into the smothering.
They were here forever
before the dust
unknowable—they have not
changed.

The sea itself
glowering
its enormous heart,
thundering in a watery grave—
these roars are
unromantic
moans
alien
as a world of three suns.

The sea refuses dust.

Soaking and blowing
pulling away,
the bones it carries
are salted, weighty
sucked off.

It is its own harshness and
dank.
Our blood
our hair
our eyes and origin
our sex—
more secret
than the
motes made up
though we turn back
to ground—
if you kiss
any of us
deeply
there is
a taste of earth.

Night Up With Nancy

Morning
low on the grassland, like your voice
smokey,
sun in
from the sea.

Except that this is
a harbor town,
it is like any dawn
I've stepped into,
still wrapped around

the dream of all-night-talk,
nightgowned gossip, blurred yawn
the eyes too heavy
to shield themselves
exploded secrets and I'm back to twelve.

This is not how I'd plan it.

This is not how I would
plan it—
lovers spun out
unwound read off
we've grown awkward as the new light
floats down.
I tell you
I've wanted to make love
in this room,
the books pressing benedictions
on our heads,
wanted to place
lit candles on the rug,
take someone here—you
nod
think of your own bluesmoke hope. Nothing comes of it.

Nothing
comes of it. We hug,
asses out, the straight
woman's embrace,
you talk of cat medicine,
animals waiting,
heartpills, you are
nine hours late, your arms
full

of books, mine full
of myself, equally cumbersome;
we hug
and already
I want
to take it back, this evening filled
with story
filled like a coffeecup,
you're the last person I expected
to drain it with.

You are the last person
I expected.

I realized that, sitting
sipping this first coffee
Of the day
watching the brooding sun
lose its battle to the mist.
Redwing blackbirds rise
and I eat this mass
of food;
there are some hungers
I cannot fill. Spaces
left
always empty.
Spaces always empty,
you said you had no more loneliness,
we've all created
ourselves, this dream,
no reality where the night ends, as if I
could take comfort in that,
no need
of flesh, the hotpress

and berryrush—instead,
a paper
I won't read,
the sizzle of bacon
and drowned music.

Drowned music.

How many nights
have I spent
listening
to orchestrated hearts; two women
singing to each other,
hands on hands, lips to thighs,
the taste that is
melody, this familiar counterpoint
presto—
you who don't smoke lighting another cigarette
it's not sex or maybe, even, a kind of love,
but there is
that dull drum,
the heart the heart,
reminding me
of the night's past music.

The past night a kind of music.

Maybe. Low clouds roll
across empty farmroads.
On the hill driving down
it's as if an icy wind pushes snow
a squall they call it where I'm from—
memory of New York and Boston
upstate just before spring—
other farmlands always driving,

rushing toward women
who moved me
more
or less
than you. There was love.
No doubt,
there was.

Today
our daylit faces in place,
you start your separate car
drive off toward the comfort
of needy cats, a beachhouse,
plants that need watering.
I am slower,
ease out of the alley
down the road toward breakfast
empty
as your bed. Your arms.

I'll buy a toothbrush, change
my shirt, arrive
an hour early for work,
the scent of your smoke and perfume
still
on my skin, up close, the scent
of the night.
Up close
it's all the same; we are
each other, we are
the rest, today
I'll spend the morning
trembling.

It will not be
from lack
of
sleep.

Paperweight
(for the Gypsy)

Janie picked up the paperweight,
the one you gave me last Christmas,
she said
it was the most beautiful thing in the room.
She cupped it like an egg
in her palm
and turned her face away
when I talked about you.

No one had ever given me
such a gift—
the night sky caught in glass;
Vincent's screaming heaven—
my own flying dreams, the weight of you...
I carried that orb as if it were my child,
over an entire country
to a city of angels
I carried it packed like a bomb in my suitcase,
sure
it would go off.

Miles now from the nearest winter,
I spend January under rain,

cactus blooms below me, there are orange trees
and the Golden State is the road
I take home.
I hold that opaque egg of who we were
remembering how you looked
as you handed it to me,
unhatched memory, a week past Christmas,
pressing it to my ear,
the geese come back,
your lovesounds,
the sighing,
of fir and oak,
the snap
of ice
and crusted cover
of a New York
snow.

Biography

Texas,
you carry Wild West complete with the Alamo
in your eyes,
no surrender never.
Watching you
I taste that salted spill,
realize
it's my own pulse my own heart
smashing staccato tattoo

Texas,
you hooked me with the first
line thrown past
those honey-lipped lonesome
coyote tales,
the red dust, blinding cold,
shitkicking bars kicking the shit
out of your soul,
so much soul I find
myself reeling in to give you room

Texas,
you've come forty-five years
from some damned cowpie town
past the Panhandle west,
paying your dues
in blood, always
paying...
There is a poem that says
such joy, such joy felt
it is like two rivers
meeting   deep in the ocean—
when I'm with you close,
always, Texas,
There is a taste
of the
sea.

Robin Podolsky

Funny Picture

Four white people in Chinatown. A handsome family.
Young parents, comfortable in their collages of Jordache,
Sergio Valente and Espirit; pastels for her, navy blue and
white for him. Two daughters, somewhere between eight
and ten.

Pause for a family photograph. Father pulls a rickshaw.
Mother on the seat, next to the oldest girl; the littlest sitting
alone on the steps near her mother's feet.

The young one is piquant in short skirt and black tights. Her
daddy is handsome and fleshy, with a lazy twisted smile.
Father and daughter meet the camera with fortress eyes.
They wear look-alike Chinese straw hats.

Mother stretches her mouth for the camera. Hers is a broad
face, decorated with a touch of pink lipstick. Her muscular
legs are clasped tight under her stiff corduroy skirt. Mother
and the oldest girl twirl a parasol together. This daughter is
sweet and vague in puffed sleeves and a jumper.

The father has paid a young man from the neighborhood
one dollar to take this picture. Now he addresses the photographer, a seventeen year old punker in a Circle Jerks t-shirt.

"So you would be a 'Chinese-American,' is that right?" The
father retains his self-consciously ironic smile as he asks this
question in tones so arch and knowing as to imply some
secret significance to it that only he and the young man

understand. The teenager raises the corners of his lips. "Sure. What kind of American are you?"

Daddy lifts an eyebrow at his family. Mother inserts an answer. "Oh, we're just regular." Her voice is high and quick.

The regular American family has come from the midwest to Los Angeles on vacation. They are trying to get away from the shadow that congests their house. The trip was conferred on the children, and prepared for, with much determined anticipation.

The little girl who sits alone knows that the shadow has followed them. She hears it whisper about her trouble, knows that her mother hears it also, but pretends not to.

This little one is bright and bitter. She plays the star. Demands things. She travels in new clothes, because she refused her sister's outgrown dresses in language so vicious that the older girl cried.

The picture is ready. Daddy looks first, then passes it around. He pushes up the corner of his eyes. "Ah so," he says. "Ah so."

Disgust conquers the last of the forgotten teenager's amusement. He offers the calm observation, "Dickhead." And walks away.

The father's ears throb red. His eyes, wild, dart to those of his wife. Her clenched face warns him. The children hold still, scanning their parents for clues. In silence, the family rearranges its posture to erase the disturbance.

The couples separate. Mother draws her firstborn to a
window display of enameled miniatures and jade trees.
Side by side, they stare into the lifeless paradise, the mother
smoothing her daughter's long straight hair.
Daddy snatches his girl off the ground and rides her on his
shoulders. He points out all the sights — big brass tigers,
paper lanterns and a Buddhist priest in long grey robes on a
visit from Japan.

"Look at the Chinaman, honey!" He squeezes her thigh and
shakes it hard. "Look at the funny man!"

The little girl sits upright, rigid and silent as the stone
Buddhas on display. Her father marches buoyantly through
the crowd, holding her ankles, her thin legs spread
around his ears.

Testimony

In October of 1981 a nineteen-year-old Lesbian named
Stephanie Reithmiller was kidnapped by a trio of "deprogrammers" who had been hired by her parents. Stephanie
was taken by force from Cincinnati to Alabama where she
was held prisoner for a week. She was deprived of food and
sleep, subjected to three "deprogramming" sessions a day
and raped repeatedly. Her father drove the kidnap vehicle.
Both parents knew that their daughter was being raped.
Stephanie's mother testified in court to having wondered
when the deprogrammers would "get down to business."
    When Stephanie was released, she returned to Cincin-
nati and filed charges against her parents and the deprogrammers. The trial prosecutor took pains to express his
sympathy with the parents and his abhorrence of homosexu-
ality. No guilty verdicts were reached. All but two of the

defendants were acquitted, and the jury deadlocked only on
the question of charging them with abduction. All sexual
battery charges were dismissed by the judge.

no one says it didn't happen

twelve people that we might sit next to on the bus
watch bathing their faces in sunlight
give directions to on the street

smelled smoke on the hair
of a woman returned from Hell
heard how the righteous became their own demons
found a reason to let the torturers go free

this is where we have to live our lives

what did those twelve imagine as they heard the evidence
what did they hear when the verdict was read
what did they go home and tell their daughters they'd done

what was Stephanie's father thinking in that house in
Alabama
did he stay and listen
did he stroke his dick

what did Stephanie's mother think about
waiting alone   wondering when they'd get down to business
was she jealous

this is where we have to live our lives
when my own parents were my age   that short a time ago
our enemies got down to business
they put pink triangles on our arms
starved and used our bodies

burned the evidence

there had been laws against such things

my friend Renee is ten years older than me
she has friends her own age who have no teeth because
they were beaten by cops as they came out of
Lesbian bars in Boston
one woman she knows was pulled into a car full of men
she escaped by throwing herself through the windshield
not even a generation ago

this is where we have to live our lives

any day   the fist in the face   teeth ripping tongue
behind any set of eyes
the prison guard look   the concentration camp look
it's nothing personal
they share the joke with you

absurd today
the idea of cattlecars

they would have to keep it a secret
someone would say something

it already happened to one of us
it wasn't kept a secret

everyone found out that they came with their van
and took a woman away
everyone was told that they starved and used her body
the evidence was burned alive
in a court of law

twelve people had nothing to say

there are laws against such things

Feasting On Coherence
for Janice

We sit on the floor
like children and crush
mouthfuls of breakfast
between teeth and tongue.
The kitten assails my toes.

I cooked
Bleu cheese eggs.
Home fries, lavish
with peppers and tomatoes.
Potatoes are my favorite food.
I snuck extra
onto your plate.

The carpet fluffs up clean,
except for your daughters' toys,
leavings of some bright plastic bloom.
Clothes sit folded in patient stacks.
Roaches are scared off.
It was different before you came.

Soon, you'll be off
to phone our neighbors into action
so that a Salvadoran child
whose eyes, dark as your daughters', are eighty years old,
can grow to some being other

than compost for Folger's Coffee.
I'll try to bring our Gay
March on Washington
home with words.

For now
the kitten takes my instep
with strategy. I savor
the final crunch of potato,
your eyes that wash my belly
with memories of your tongue,
that future of peace and plenty
we've conjured gently
home to us
this morning.

Choices

i saw a film
of a real massacre today
a priest in El Salvador
had been murdered by the government
because he called for
land to the poor
for democracy
because
he didn't stick to
irreproachable generalities

he talked about
North American multinational corporations
that profit from a cash crop economy

owned by 14 families
so Archbishop Oscar Romero
was shot in the chest
as he prayed

his funeral became a demonstration
thousands of people in the streets
sang to the memory of Archbishop Romero
swore vengeance on his killers
in voices heavy with patient rage

soldiers surrounded the square
the first shots rumbled out
the crowd was so big
a lot of people stood confused for minutes
as others screamed and fell

i wondered if i would know what to do in a massacre
real footage of war always looks so aimless
not like the movies
where everybody charges ahead in one direction

some people ran into buildings and looked out
others dropped to the ground
and rolled away to escape the shooting
some stayed
to pick up the wounded
they joined hands
to make human stretchers and
carried them off

so there were choices
even in a massacre

everybody looked ordinary

even the brave ones with the wounded
their foreheads were pinched and anxious
their mouths slack
hair clumped up into funny shapes

i saw a movie today
of a real massacre
smeared twisted mouths of crying children
smashed open bodies
looked just like the meat at the store
dead eyes held no answers
captives filed by
under the guns
hands on their heads

in a real country
where ordinary people
do heroic things
because their children go hungry
while good land is planted up
with cotton, coffee and sugar
for the profit of
North American multinational corporations
because they each know somebody who was killed for
complaining
or for nothing
and they just can't take anymore

see we're already in a war
and nobody asked us
if we wanted to be in it
or which side we wanted to be on

the President
wants to send more money and guns

to the government of El Salvador
he wants to send young men
who have joined our army
because they can't find jobs
in an economy run
by multinational corporations

their eyes are mostly dark
their skin is mostly brown
like that of the ordinary heroes
who ran and died in the square
like that of the girls and boys
with soft frightened eyes
who survived
who are learning to shoot
who will be waiting
for the marines
with brown skin and soft frightened eyes
who will be sent to kill them
so that
North American multinational corporations
can continue to profit
from the coffee cotton and sugar
that starves children

i remember another war
they didn't bother to ask us
if we wanted to be in

we were fighting then
for zinc rubber and tin
and to make an example
of a dark-eyed nation
which resisted the government of generals
owned by

North American multinational corporations

i remember what happened
when we said no

i remember paralyzed veterans
beaten by police in the streets

Ruben Salazar
a Chicano journalist
shot to death by police in his own barrio

the rifles
of national guardsmen

i remember
that just a few times
the everyday of darkeyed peoples overseas
of Los Angeles barrios
walked out of the six o'clock news
shattered the dreams of Gold Star mothers
visited state campuses
became our massacre

i remember that there were some
who ran away and never looked back
some who stayed with the wounded
who joined hands
and carried them to safety
a few who never made it home

there are choices
even in a massacre
even for ordinary people
like me

Paula Gunn Allen

Arousings

1.

clear the ditch
the roadway.
get them freed and long,
walk alongside them watch
water running
clear and frothy, cold.
let the rain
in through the pores
let it wash clear the pane,
let the air in, break
the glass, stay within the bounds
of reason, loading up with things
lovely and necessary, things
that are dry, things that are lost.
go away from meaning into longing.
go far and long, go wide, go deep, go on.
let the craft go on pitching
on the highhigh waves,
let it cast the winds away, let
the rain go down the face, the trunk,
the body's limbs, let it roar and tumble,
let the wind wash clear
the dire spaces, all disease,
the tall twisted places of the dark,
the Roman arches, the Goths and Visigoths,
the slaughter.
let the water drench with laughter,

with what there is that's cool,
with what there is that's sweet.
at Laguna in the proper season
they clean the ditches.
so life bearer will freely pour.
they call it wonder.
water.
they call it thought.
they call it peaceful hearts
and sharing. caring. caring for.

2.

across the emptiness of gray
spray of rain on the highway
becoming your face,
across the moisture-laden miles
the hills pouring with her sweat
her grateful tears of release
recognition, recognized
see her, how she rises
her breath frothy deep on the air
her gasping, her need:
she has a new lover this year.
have you noticed how wet
she's becoming, how erratic?
she smiles and roars,
pours in perfect passion
tosses her hair, body,
her legs,
she claps her hands, she sings.
she dances.
the grandlady, so fine this year,
this season, this solstice, this
solace, this spring.

and your eyes gray reflect her joy
they glow like miles at sea, like rising
fog. i think of her touch,
your hands
subtle and quick.
i think of small furry creatures, ferret, raccoon.
of how you spit and hissed the first year through,
how you bit me then:
tiny sharp teeth baring
so lately let free from the cage
of mortality.   of your fear.
i think of how you loved.
desperately.

    3.

how you loved me. made love to me.
what i saw there when i was held.
in the wild tangle of our tongues' necessity,
rooting in softleafed places,
melting and pouring like the hills today,
ground gone to water, running toward the sea,
heat rising but not in rage.
in love.
just the seagray of your gaze,
your longing, arms raised to clasp
me,
  in sight
       of the Woman
    she
       lying in a pond
              in the woods
  in the pond of her self,
              her dreams.
  lying breathless, she.

taken with a dream
a sighting
of her lovely lover
             who is coming down,
                          running, down
to meet her where she's waiting
   in her pond, in her lake, in her sea.
we could see her waiting
             for the time to be
                          her time.
      her arms ready to rise
      her knees beginning to open, to lift,

we said: she's waking to love.
after so long a time
the sleeping one awakens.
what will that mean?
looking long into each others eyes,
the question spun between us,
glimmered in the softlight,
thoughts, butterflies, moths, soft wings dipping
between our lips, our eyes:

                   know this:
      the woman of the earth.
      the woman of the sky.
      the woman of the water,
      of the seaspray.
      the fog.
      wakes.

will pour down
                   in the mountain soil.
will descend
                   on the limbs of fallen trees.

will blow free
                    in the sleet,
                              the blizzard winds
wrapped in white   as becomes one   just awakened.

          the woman of the hives, of the bees;
          the woman of the cocoon, the butterflies;
          the woman of the coiling meanders, the time;
          the woman of the snaking fires, the flame;
          the woman of the water, the snow, the rain.

the woman whose waking means
wonder.
water.
want and need.
and her awakening is not death or war, not rage.
she's in love, that woman the world. she's in love.

Chaney Holland

The Furies
a novella excerpt

*THE FURIES is a prose/poetry novella that centers
around one person's need for commitment versus an artist's
need for freedom. The narrator is in California, recalling
events that took place in Venice, Italy, during the past year,
involving her and her lover, Cypris; Vahanian, Cypris' art
teacher and Sergei, Cypris' male lover.*

*Enigmatic and seductive, this excerpt reflects the narra-
tor and her view of the world. Her recollections are feverish,
potent, desultory, her mood uneasy. She seeks coherence and
finds it is always infused with her own form of fatalism..*

California

I THOUGHT AT FIRST they were voices speaking to me.
Something pricking my ears to an agonizing sound. Wild
dogs howling from the hills at night, seemingly savage and
frenzied with grief. A highpitched hum I began to hear
through my fingertips. On a clear afternoon, a lone coyote
darted into the path of my car. For an instant, askew from his
paralyzed body, his narrow skittish head turned towards me.
I pulled over to the roadside and stood trembling over him
until I was able to carry the scrawny body from the pool of
blood spreading on the hot asphalt. I laid him among the
carmine blossoms of the ice plants covering the cliff and left
quickly.

There is something waiting, just ahead on the road. At
that instant,   I waited for the coyote's scream and heard
myself listening to another cry. A desolate half-moan, unhu-
man, the sound of some unspeakable deprivation. I pulled the

thick cotton sheets closer until they were limp with the sweat of my fear. Then rose andwent barefoot and naked through the darkened rooms.

Cypris was crouched over a letter, immersed in a past we never knew had existed. I held my dry hand to her feverish head. Her studio was suffocatingly hot. In the slatted light, the chimera Sergei had made irradiated dimension and power. The huge, clumsy bird hung in the darkest corner of the room. Its double beaked heads jutted from the heavy, stuffed body. Claws and fleshy wings extended as though it were about to spring. I remember how it grew in the night and permeated the room so that it was difficult to breathe. We had returned from a few unhappy weeks in Rome. There was a letter from Vahanian's lover though we had not known there was a lover. Afterwards, Cypris insisted that she had killed him. Vahanian died of a brain aneurism in California months before. No one had written so we never heard. She came to believe that she had drawn too much from him to deluge her canvases with gold, with god. That he had allowed this because as protegee and mentor they magnified a shared sphere of imagination.

After I left Venice, she wrote that she was with him almost constantly. She could have been his child, though he was younger than our parents. The same round blue staring eyes, an odd way of turning to meet you. As though shifting from a faraway perspective to view only the unfamiliar. Suddenly, you would be disconcerted, embarrassed as though exposed. And they occupied space in a realm of singular possibilities. In Venice, she seemed like a gold mosaic figure drifting from and into the Byzantine walls. I came to know such potent ghosts by tracing her distraught path into the side worlds. Down narrow stone corridors to the sea I lost all sense of time.   And in everything that followed I was a passive observer, at times her accomplice. There had been ample warning of disaster, her depression the previous win-

ters, the all-consuming work. But my desire singed and
chafed like hers until I satisfied it. We were endlessly caught
in this bind, burning both ends, watching time run out.

Most people kept their distance from Vahanian without
ever knowing why. He never gave much away and we knew
nothing of his life beyond the university. In appearance he
resembled a weathered sea-captain, pot-bellied, bandy-
legged, true blue eyes. He had strange habits, shamanistic.
His hands were antennas to the world. In the morning he
made his customary approach toward one of the four walls
covered with drawings. Fingers sensing and with slow deliberation impressing tacks into the boards. We sat absolutely
still, upright, until she released a small moan as he drove the
tack in. We were favored though she was the ingenue, she
understood what all the other students did not. She never
failed him. I felt no jealousy. Painting was magic, but not my
magic. Straining to see, I was caught between his vision and
the knowledge of her long legs, deliciously bare beneath our
table. Lost the breath of him through the curve of her thighs
disappearing in folds of lavender cloth. Confusing her with
him. We went on for a year like this. I did not dream of light
as she did. Though light was turning in on itself, irradiating
me, with and without volition.

What does it mean that we were not enough for each
other? We were innocent in the old life. There were personal
betrayals in Venice. And yet, who betrayed whom, or was it
suddenly when we heard the sharp intake of our breath. The
thump of the ouija board. When it was too late to stop the
voices. Yes, the withering air of that summer, the Erinyes
close at our heels. The rest is unclear to me. Cypris had no
real wish to escape its vortex since it gave birth to and
sustained the ravenous appetite of her art. I fled after only
three months.

Venezia

I let her sleep on the floor, hid the letter behind the chimera. Chanting softly to myself, I waited. But it was she who woke me. No moon after the harsh sweating day. The wind was warm and blowing hard. We went to the far end of the Punta della Dogana until the way ended abruptly at sea. The great stone cathedral loomed above us, the water slapped against the bank and spilled over. I leaned against the wall to steady myself. She took no notice of our wet clothing or of me. She began to step around the corner on the low frieze. I followed, hands searching the smooth stone for a hold. A wave soaked my legs as the hot wind drove us against the wall. She moved much more quickly, her wet body glittering in the darkness. There were dark stains on my fingers where they gripped between the blocks. I pressed my lips to the church as though stone might embrace me.

Around the corner, stairs cut into the wall face led to a small opening. I turned and looked at the black water below us. We turned and crouched as we passed through. Water seeped through the walls and made pools on the floor. Candlelight ahead. As we descended, the air chilled me. I thought Sergei must have brought her this way before. Beyond the door, she stared at the altar. Its red velvet cloth dimly glowed in the vast chasm. I saw a high priest step out of darkness, the sacrificial knife slicing through the air above him. There was nothing. Only my uneven breathing which no longer belonged to me. *He's dead,* I said weakly when she pulled me down with her. I saw apparitions, black feet standing beside me. Cowled forms hovering above, voices whispering names I didn't know. *Someone has a knife*, I said to her. She never heard. I couldn't move. The sound of water running. I said, *it will reach us*. She held me on the marble. In the night, I dreamed my mother came. She wrapped me in paper to soak up my sweat and life. Her bones were stiff and crackling. She said she was grieving. We crept out of the Salute church at dawn.

● ● ● ● ● ● ● ● ● ● ● ● ●

THE FUMES FROM MARGHERA made me sick that afternoon. I lay on the mattress coughing, my breath coming in short gasps followed by a high frightening wheeze. She went back and forth from her studio bringing hot lemon water, bathing my face with damp rags. Her eyes were distant, pre-occupied with the synthetic space of her most recent canvas. There was nothing that could be done anyway. Several times a year the attacks were violent enough to resist any form of medication. Perhaps the factories at Marghera were spewing some unusually virulent poison that day, and I was the indicator, the body chosen to decipher its corrupt tongue. Often the most severe allergic reactions occurred at random in an air-conditioned room or high desert in the winter. To despair or fight was only further aggravation. The end eventually led into a long, deep sleep. My mother, who scorned any form of ill-ness, had viewed these attacks with contempt and dis-belief. In time I came to accept them as a purging of body and mind. Something given to me, a paradoxical release of pain, like childhood nightmares.

In the evening she left her work to lie down with me, supporting my body with hers, holding my head so I was able to breathe more easily. I pressed her hand between my breasts as though it would help aspirate my lungs. During the night I woke several times choking. She wanted to take me to the nearby ospedale then, but I protested, knowing it would pass. She told me a dream in the way people feel compelled to when they first wake. *I saw my hip bones and femur where the flesh from the hips and thighs had been removed. I looked at all my bones and tendons, thought it odd that I was missing all this flesh. The flesh from the back of my hips had also been been hollowed out. My hips fascinated me. The*

*bones fascinated me as usual--and it was quite grotesque--
but somehow disguised because there was a flap of flesh on
each thigh and around the hips that covered huge gaping
trenches. So that when you looked at it you might not see the
bones.* I began to cry. She held me closer. *I'm sorry*, I said,
I don't know why I'm crying.

At dawn, I was released. I sat very still, breathing carefully, grateful to feel the even rush of air. Her mouth was
slightly open, arms around me like the long night we took the
train from Amsterdam to Venice. A journey that so ex-
hausted us that we alternately dozed in one another's arms,
waking in sudden starts as the train pulled into each station.
That trip took on significance now, the margin between the
old life I had known and the life I had thought to make with
her. She had said, *you don't belong here,* and it was true.
Venice was a bridge, a momentary hallucination, marking
the ancient boundary.

The several hundred miles south had drained us. We
found space in a second-class compartment and spent the
night shifting uncomfortably as the train sped across three
borders. On the horizon the liquid shapes of dusk flattened,
the whistle shrilled through the darkness. I lay in her arms
and watched the cold blue light shiver over her sleeping form.
I felt a strange excitement then, as though a new scene had
wiped across a screen. I had thrown myself clear of the past,
of the man who had held me there for so long. Now nothing
was familiar, nothing known to me. A line of perspiration
gathered between my breasts, the compartment grew stuffier.
I tipped the water bottle back and swallowed the last bit. The
woman across glanced at us and moved her bare feet farther
from the sleeping couple to her left. The man stirred and
groaned. His mouth opened as his head fell back. Cypris
woke as the train lurched and slowed to a halt. *I need water,*
she said.

In those first disorienting days I thought I'd defeated the

year that had passed between us. The airport where she'd met
me had been jammed at mid-morning. The crowd jostled its
way toward customs and spilled into the lobby. I waited by
the baggage claim in the sweltering heat, my back turned
toward the throng pressing against the glass doors. Then
stood nervously outside until I caught a glimpse of a woman
searching by the windows. In spite of the temperature, she
wore a black sweater, gold tights under short trousers. I
watched for an instant as the city clock boomed overhead.
We're older now, I thought. Cypris turned, banked through
the clouds and came out smiles. We went to the hotel and
talked for three days.

During the long night on the train, I dreamed that she was
streaming with indigo color, leaving thick viscous streaks
across our bodies. I woke to find hands coaxing the damp
hair from my forehead. My sense of time lapsed into inter-
vals of motion, then cessation. She slept in resistance to the
monotony. We hardly spoke. When I did, the words
crumbled from my mouth like a stutterer's, decaying in the
atmosphere of acrid sweat. In the early morning, we reached
the coast and crossed the Ponte Della Liberta to the island of
Venezia. As the train crawled the bridge, Cypris pointed to
the industrial filth, like a grey cloud city in the dawn's haze.
Marghera will spoil Venice before it has a chance to sink, she
said. When we reached the train station, our fatigue was
overwhelming. The steps and courtyard were littered with
the sleeping bodies and backpacks of summer travelers. We
took the vaporetto through the Grande Canal, only the suit-
cases wedged on either side and her steadying hand kept me
upright. Gold light from the city and water colored the dark
space behind my closed eyes. I asked for the time. She said 6
a.m. How could it be so hot at dawn? No breeze, the absolute
stillness of this morning, gold shadows darting across my
face. The vaporetto slipped under the last bridge, enclosing us
in a savagely beautiful gold. I did not open my eyes again.

I followed her off the ferry and through a narrow cobbled street, the wheeled luggage grinding over the pavement behind me. The high confining walls emitted a damp, hoary odor, the light struck harshly as we came into a great still courtyard. *It's midday, everyone sleeps,* she explained over her shoulder. Each breath seemed to drag heavily in the torpid air, I saw my boots were coated with a layer of chalky dust. A sense of the city's oppressiveness enveloped me, the unbroken facade of burnished gold and copper buildings. It was as though no other place existed or we now existed in fourth-dimensional time. Through the end of a long passageway I caught a glimpse of an empty gondola sailing past and stopped momentarily. Cypris ran her hand over the blackened face of a bull on the wall and slipped her fingers through the nose ring. Her eyes found mine sympathetically. *We're almost there,* she said.

THE BELL WOKE ME in the afternoon. My skin felt dirty and sweaty and I did not attempt to move. I sensed what had been the darkness and heat lingering in the sheets crumpled at my feet. Cypris was gone. The vague sound of voices filtered into the room, bare of furniture save for the mattress and a mirror. When I turned on my side, I saw the yellow tulips and amaryllis in a clear green glass on the floor. One flower was open. I raised my head and gazed into the center. Six amaranth spears ringed the yellow anther. The inner walls were stained with the impression of fine hairs where the spears had once bruised purple pigment. In that dirty, hot room I felt something like joy begin a tremulous movement and surge through my body. It was unlike so many false starts in the past. Lovers who had the sensation of an artificial high, the shock of nicotine to the lungs. Expansion, seizure, and then the familiar ending of suppressed emotion. I waited for the feeling to submerge, but it welled again.

I rose and reached for my clothes, wanting to find her, but

faltered for a moment. On the corner of the far wall, Sergei's chimera had appeared, its puffy drab form strung by rusted nails. A half-smoked cigarette smoldered on the windowsill below. Unwillingly, I went closer and stretched my hand out to touch one of the monstrous faces. In the mirror, the backs of two more heads emerged from the torso. One face was bare and featureless but the one I touched had a necklace of barbed wire. Gold leaf lined the eyes, the eyelashes were iridescent bronze and thick as though mascara had been applied. It had the effect that a transvestite does, both hilarious and fearful.

The boy in Los Angeles lying half in the gutter, half on the cub. A black cocktail dress torn and slashed at the waist. Early morning on Santa Monica Boulevard, the Latinos gathered at the corner waiting for the car of the man who would give them work. His face was bleeding color, blue mascara, crimson rouge, he was weeping. His black filmy stockings were dirty, the heel was torn from one pump. A filthy parrot, a disgraced peacock. Behind him, the bar was hermetically sealed against the daylight. The Latinos stared or ignored him. No one approached. The sun was dark and hot. A wave of nausea soaked me. I knelt down to touch her shoulder and the sky fired blood-red. My powder-white shirt, the melting sky of searing black above the concrete slabs, the purple bruises on her raw flesh. I prayed for fire in August. He closed his eyes against the flame and I stared into the chimera.

In her bedroom I was acutely aware of the strong odor of turpentine and paint. It distracted me from another smell, faint but tangible. At first I could not find its origin. I touched the palm of my hand to my cheek and snatched it away. It was something I hadn't known before. The smell of another woman. I looked down at my bared feet and legs, the soft sloping ridge where my hip curved into my pelvis. Then raised my head and met my startled eyes in the mirror.

After a long, hot shower I let the cold water run over my

body until I cooled down. When I joined Cypris and Sergei, my clothes were damp with perspiration. He looked at me curiously, extending his hand politely. He was younger than I'd expected, younger than I. Also a student at the Accademia though he studied with Clementi. Cypris leaned back against the stove, stretching her long legs and taking small sips of espresso. Her eyes were narrowed and preoccupied. She poured coffee for me and filled the rest of the cup with steamed milk. They resumed their conversation in Italian. Sergei had tight black curls, a wide sensitive face. Tiny wry lines traveled from the corners of his mouth. He'd brought slides of new paintings. She was waving her hand in the air, talking in a low determined voice. He threw up his hands helplessly and said the Italian word for Russian, Ruski. *They're cheating you,* Cypris said furiously. He shrugged.

He didn't know I was coming or how long I would stay. He seemed distant. She didn't tell me he was staying. That was her way. I was too hot to move. The neighbors were repairing their boat outside. Sergei left for the afternoon. I was asleep in the studio when he rang again. He had a message from his friend Zhou. He wanted her to go to Rome, I was invited. The long journey from Holland had tired me and we had had only one night in Venice. But she wanted to go and I acquiesced to please her.

Later she told me she never would have touched me if I hadn't reached out first. It absolved her from any blame. It made our desire my vocation. She told me I could go if I wanted, that my unhappiness was unbearable to her. Beyond the social amenities she abhorred any moral restrictions. It was a sign of weakness to her, of complacency with a world she viewed as increasingly ugly and brutal. She slept with him that night and afterwards, every night he was with us.

Armi per sporti. A burly soccer player points a hunting rifle at the camera and winks. Guns for sport. The screen

flickers and a young housewife holds out a brand of contra-
ceptives. Cypris flicks her cigarette butt at the tv, sits up on
her elbows and imitates the woman's ingratiating tone. These
commercials are the only sponsors for *The Alfred Hitchcock
Hour* and run at least ten times a night. *Guns and birth
control,* Cypris says, *fabulous.* She cocks her finger at the
soccer player and blows him away.

The mattress is dirty and stained with cigarettes and
lemon gelato. I no longer take the sheets to the laundry or
enjoy the starched feel of clean linen. The television flattens
our image so that we appear as small boys in cotton under-
wear. Since we heard of Vahanian's death, she only wants to
watch tv or sleep. I don't feel it as she does, though I also
began drawing with him. She tells me she's glad I'm here,
that no one else would understand what his loss means. In the
afternoons Sergei comes to visit. He and I sit together in the
tiny kitchen. We converse in German, mine from high
school, his learned as a child from Russian comic books.
Cypris ignores him. When he leaves, her long fingers find
mine. In the gold night, I pray fire will take him. By day,
hiding in the cool house, she shears my head to a soft thick
down, rubs her feet in my shorn locks. Often I am numb with
happiness.

My books are piled beside the bed. I've abandoned them,
forgotten that I am doing nothing here. Though I don't
realize any change in myself, something has been decided. I
have only to endure the heat. It's the way back that con-
sumes, overwhelms me. Each morning I cross the Ponte di
Vecchio to buy a paper, anticipating the bloody headlines. To
feel confirmed in my fear and the sudden sickness that came
this morning. JAL fell out of the sky like a winged bird. She
calculates for me. They're going down at the rate of one
every six weeks so I only have to make certain I fly in
between times. On the flight over I dreamed the nose of
another jet tore through the passenger area and paused a

fraction before my eye. The gleaming stripe across its bulging side pinned me, air stung my eyes and I waited. As though watching a water bubble caught against a faucet tap. Waiting forever for its fall.

I read and discuss in morbid detail how it fell. I see the white body of the plane disintegrating, breaking apart as easily as clouds. Once when were were flying over France one of the twin engines burst into flame. From the window I saw black smoke over the left wing. She held my hand and seeing my terror said, *There's nothing we can do. Why do you always fight?* Because the plane is a wounded bird plummeting to earth, because when something falls from the sky we are being warned. I tell her I smell death in the air. This pleases her, it confirms her suspicions. The gods are not easily appeased. After the earthquakes in California, their anger lingers for days and weeks. Above Sunset and Alvarado, people sleep in the streets. Their children lie on cardboard beds by the front yard dumpsters. The women wait beneath multi-colored beach umbrellas; their men sleep in a blue van. When they finally return to their homes, the after shock comes at 4 a.m. The people stream from their slum houses into the streets of giant uprooted palms. The pillars shift and the houses sags. Later, the Santa Anas will drive a frond into my bedroom window and cover me with shattered glass. There will be no blood, but the memory will resurface. The gods are never appeased.

In the warm lamplight, she takes the paper from me and throws it away. She knows I prefer to remain close by, on the edge where I can see. When the time comes, I can jump either way. Nothing prevents catastrophe. Tonight we're safe in this small, dark cocoon. Our breath is smoke around our heads, we are sleeping.

Marlene Pearson

To Document A 20-Second Hug Between 2 Women In A Mental Hospital w/o Saying The "L" Word

Mark saw it next
grabbed a pen/ wrote what he'd watched

this time one finger on a stop watch
eyes slit-visioned behind glassed-in desk

11:30 pm/ Joline came out
of her room/ me from mine/ Mark spied

the quiet way we came into each other's arms
there in the hall and hugged again

whole paragraphs seeping through fingertips
our language elemental as touch
we were like one flesh
2 heads/ 4 legs in 2 pair of pajamas

some monster he thought
it scared him

11:45pm/ Mark put down my chart
filled his coffee cup and looked out
at the full moon

we knew he watched/ staff always watched
but I didn't know he counted seconds

drew a face/ marked an "x" on the spot
where I kissed her cheek
when Dr. G. squirmed in his chair
the next morning/ asked how long it
lasted/ did I really kiss her/ where?

I said let's define this thing
we hug because we are alike
2 women needing arms that know
that hold on tight/ we're so alike when she cries/
I cry too and our tears taste the same
they taste of the same salt

so what is it, doctor?
a 10 second hug—intense friendship
a 15 second hug—questionable behavior
a 20 second hug—abnormal/ red light red light
is that right?

well, it was 20 seconds/ maybe more
and you did not say the word

I could not say the word/ I was still
caught in your ward
but I wanted to

I wanted to kiss her and hug her
like the "L" word
like a Lesbian.

A Woman Who Loves A Woman

I tried to draw your face
the day before I left the hospital
so you would never be away from me.
A woman who loves a woman.

I packed the cafeteria salt/paper shakers,
3 glasses & 2 coffee cups & asked Alice,
the cook, to bake an extra dozen bran muffins
for me to take home in a plastic bag.

At home I kept them frozen so they'd last.
When I heated one I could see you walk
through the cafeteria door to our table, the one
in the corner, where we met most every morning
at 7 that whole year.

When I bit into the muffin its warm smell
reminded me of trees, of the park where we met.
How long's your pass, I asked.

Not long enough, and so you danced.
Balleted on grass velvet, music
in your ears, while I wrote it all
down so it would never be away
from me.

Washing the crumbs down the sink I remember
how you left the park, old feelings, that bad
ghost chained to your heel, following too close.
You headed for Von's, downed cookies,
M&MS, then threw up until
the whole
day was gone.

I wasn't free either. My censor slipped into my car
when I did, to drive back. She would not
stop whispering in my ear, and so I didn't eat.
I grew so thin I couldn't see myself.

When they weighed me I stuffed
nickels, quarters, pennies in my pockets,
wore 3 sweaters, 2 pair of jeans, just to stay
above 99. Just to keep my pass
with my daughter.

Though I knew when I saw Melinda she'd cry.
She always cried when we picked up the crayons,
put the paper away and I drove her back home
away from me.

The muffins are gone, but I am just now remembering
how I wanted your hugs to be, how I wanted you
the way I wasn't supposed to, the way guilt
sat on my shoulder, shook a finger into my ear and dared
me to eat. I starved in their values.

A censor held my key. I thought
she swallowed it. It has taken me
years to get it back. Begin
to make my own definitions.

This morning I found flour in my cupboard. I have written
my own recipe, baked muffins and invited you
over to eat with me.

Carol Schmidt

Friends

I know you well
and now I know you more.
You've unfolded your personality to me
And now you've let me open those lovely folds
Of soft dark skin and rest my chin
And feel your gentleness turn turgid and build
A new Central Nervous System
To wrest feeling from your mind.
You've let me find the jumpy spots
Where my fingernails are painful
And let me run my fingernails to the edges of those areas
So you've writhed in pleasure bordering pain.
You've let me intuit where to let my hand flow and slow.
You've let me find the softness and hardness of your body,
Even where they differ from what the softness and hardness
of your soul
Would lead me to expect.
You've let me probe your body armor and find its
weaknesses.
You've let me discover how your breasts
Are like licking a silver teaspoon of apricot brandy,
The chaser after savoring a rounded stonewear mug of
apricot nectar.
You've let me taste your special flavor of homemade yogurt.
You've let me trace your scars,
The visible remnants of how your body once suffered
And was found imperfect and external healers forced their
way in
With your grogged permission.

You've let me compare the reality of your
nearly perfect body
With the pronouncements of your nearly perfect
nutrition plan,
And you let me handle my fears and painful recognition
That my lifestyle gives me away once unclothed,
And you trusted me to survive the comparison
Without a word.
You've let me taste your sweat,
Like coming up for life after being pressured down
Into a Venice riptide and finally floating free
Once I gave up struggling,
Surfacing again in peace and freedom
And letting the Pacific trickle drip by drip on my lip as I rest,
Knowing each salty drop has the power of
the Pacific behind it.
You've let me skim your wet hair back from your face
And see your straining features with no softening frame
To lure my eyes away from your wrinkles to your curls.
You've let me find your life rhythms, which, once knowing,
I could call up again and use if I were to want to hurt you
With your own pulsations and roadmaps inward.
You've let me love you
And I do.

Maria Jose Delgado

WAITING

Waiting
thinking you've decided not
to come.

You walked through the light
my heart stopped

BARBARA

I think about
the train ride,
the beer I drank,
people I bumped,
the smiles I got.

A new city
with you — I saw
lights, buildings,
dirt and scum.

And all
was washed away.
Hot tub, sauna, and
bed.

Sweet woman, so strong

we are.
Together we could kick
the asses of five men
'cause
Junior punks, we are—
tough, mean, and brave.

ENCARRUJADA

Vino sin llamar
entro y me beso.
No se su crespo contener,
entra y sale,
vuela y recalca.
Lloramos, fumamos y nos besamos.
No se que hacer
vino hoy y se fue.

¡Mi novia! ¡Que bonita es!
con esa majestuosidad
se desliza de aqui alla
con sus carnosos labios me rodean en besos
y su pelo moreno se trenza al mio.

¡Dios mio! ¡Que malo es todo esto!
¡Que falta de practica!
¿Es la escasez de inspiracion?

No la tengo a ella.
Tan linda.
Tan real.

¡Mi novia! ¡Que bonita esta!

Sobre la almohada verde
dos cabesas como perlas litigan.
Fui fiel.   ¿Porque te marchastes?
Fui fiel.   ¿Porque me abrasastes?

ENTANGLEMENT
translated by Carmen Silva

She came without calling.
She entered and kissed me.
I cannot contain her,
in...out
in flight...submerged.
We cried, smoked, kissed.
I don't know what there is to be done.
She came today, then left.

My love is so beautiful.
There is a nobility present
that unravels with frenzied kisses surrounding me
her brown hair entwined in mine.

My God, this all seems so wrong.
Is the lack of familiarity so great?
Is such the scarcity of inspiration?

I do not have her.
So beautiful.
So real.

My love has so much beauty.
We are two heads on a green pillow.
Two heads, like pearls, on a bed of negotiation.
I was true. Why did you leave?
I was true. Why did you ever hold me?

Ayofemi Stowe Folayan

April 4, 1968

IT WAS MY SECOND semester at Vassar, and the afternoon of April 4 with its balmy spring weather invited me to grab a sketch pad and abandon the overdue assignments piled on my desk. I found a dry rock under an enormous evergreen near the golf course, where I sketched in the gift of extra daylight, surrounded by a chorus of squirrels and birds. Finally, my stomach sent out angry hunger signals for me to get back to the dormitory for dinner.

The deserted dining room startled me without its usual hum of conversations. I felt chilled by the silence as I walked the dark paneled hallway. In the lobby I turned my attention to the crowd stuffed into the tiny lounge.

At the doorway Pacey crossed the threshold, nearly knocking me aside. Her face was grey and ashen. Tension from the group clutched at my throat. Surprised by the urgency in my voice, I grabbed her arm and demanded: "What's going on? Why is everybody in here? The dining room is totally empty!" I stopped and waited, anticipating bad news.

Pacey stared at me as if I had totally lost my mind.

"Where have you been? Somebody shot Martin Luther King in Memphis. It's on the news now." I tried to decode the information as she walked toward the elevator.

"That's impossible! What are you talking about? Nobody...." The elevator door closed, leaving me to enter the overfilled lounge. Students sat in ghostly grey light, created by flickering images on an ancient black and white television. A neatly groomed newscaster dispensed the tragic details. A lump formed in my throat as the news awakened painful memories. I rushed outside to escape my surging emotions.

Memories of other painful times filled my mind. I relived the moment as a four-year-old when I awoke to an explosion and watched flames rip the wall from my house and suffocating smoke fill the air. I recalled endless replays of the horse-drawn cortege bearing John Kennedy's body through a respectful Washington. I saw news footage of clubs and dogs and fire hoses turned on people peacefully kneeling. I remember clutching my dad's hand, nearly crushed by the dense crowd but able to hear the eloquent voice of Martin Luther King, Jr. speaking in the shadow of "The Great Emancipator" on that searing August afternoon as he described his vision of equality.

Slowly I became aware of the cool night air drying the tears on my face. I couldn't imagine this gentle man violently blasted apart by assassin's bullets. Simultaneously, I felt a desire to respond to this tragedy with the same love and courage King had exemplified in his life and work.

Gentle rays of sunshine filtered through my curtains and awakened me from a restless sleep. My course of action was still unclear as I went through my morning rituals. In the shower, steaming water poured over my body, washing away my indecision and grief. I roughly dried my body and toweled away the tears on my cheeks. I kept searching my mind for the appropriate response as I absent-mindedly took three books from my desk and walked toward the lobby. Students passed me on their way to class as though nothing out of the ordinary had happened. The central quad was nearly empty when I arrived just after 8:00 a.m.

I opened the first book to page one and began to read aloud. King's articulate prose clearly explained "Why We Can't Wait" better than any arguments I could create. The consequences of my actions did not concern me; I simply kept reading. I was determined to display my devotion to the principles King had espoused. Oblivious to others around me, I read on, as a light drizzle sprinkled the growing group of listeners.

My picture appeared in the campus paper the next day, although I never noticed the photographer. The group sat respectfully as I read with intense grief, hoping to somehow assuage my guilt or restore my faith. Later, when my throat was swollen from the effort of reading, I paused to notice the students surrounding me, filling the entire quad. As the rain grew stronger, the Dean offered the college chapel. Linking arms, we sang *We Shall Overcome* as we marched across the campus.

Glendale

Judy sat at the wrought iron table in the French Market Place, talking excitedly about her apartment-hunting adventures. "I looked at the perfect place today! A little one bedroom house in Glendale, behind the landlord's place. Only two-seventy-five a month." Susan and I listened to our friend as she continued her tale. "I don't know if I'll get it though. She didn't seem to like me very much."

I thought to myself: I wonder why! I looked at Judy, with her blonde hair cut very butch, her left ear carrying three posts and an ear cuff with delicate turquoise stones, and her gold-rimmed glasses. Judy's youthful exuberance seemed almost anachronistic in the caustically cynical atmosphere of the restaurant.

She continued talking in a conversational tone. "Although, she did say that she was really glad to finally show it to somebody white. She didn't know what she was going to do, with so many Negroes interested in the place. She already had a handful of applications when I got there, and the ad just started today. People must be really desperate for apartments!" Judy said the word "Negroes" in a way that let me know it hadn't jarred her to hear it or repeat it.

I tried to think of some response to the remark, as other words tumbled past, but my mind went blank, like the television screen right after the power is turned off, with that one little dot of light at the center. I very carefully held onto my spoon, stirring the broccoli cheese soup from one side of the bowl to the other. Judy went on with her story. "She's supposed to call me back sometime later this week." Her head was angled toward Susan, whose clear beige-skinned face was surrounded by short brown hair.

I bit hard on my lip and tried nonchalantly to ask, "Where's the restroom in this place, anyway?" Tears of frustration and impotence escaped the corners of my eyes and slid down my face toward my mouth.

Judy stopped her narrative and looked over at me. "Hey! Are you okay? Here, come on, I'll show you where it is." I stumbled after her to the restroom.

A bright glare glanced off the mosaic walls of the bathroom. Gratefully, I dove into a vacant stall as the contents of my guts forced my clenched teeth apart. Tears flowed harder now, pain mixed with embarrassment. I kept thinking, "It's 1986, not 1956! How can I be hearing this?"

I came out of the stall and washed my face and hands after I rinsed my mouth. As I pulled a paper towel from the dispenser, my friend came up and gave me a long hug. "Don't take it personally," she said. "That's just the way they are in Glendale."

I nodded, knowing that she meant the last sentence to convey support. I shrugged out of her hug, and we walked back to the table. Susan waited with an anxious expression on her face. I just didn't want to talk. "I need to get out of here and pick up my daughter," I lied. I put some money on the tray holding the bill and walked away from the table without looking back.

In the car, I thought of all the things I had wanted to say. "Yes, I know how they are in Glendale! That's the city that still has a municipal law that forces black maids to be out of town by sundown! You call yourself my friend. Am I supposed to never visit you again because you've found 'the perfect little house'? I'm one of those 'Negroes' your future landlady is so terrified of. How different do you think the word 'Negro' really is from 'nigger' in her mind?" I didn't want to inspire Judy's guilt, yet my thoughts were full of anger at her betrayal.

I thought about my mother's nightly ritual of burning her ebony skin with the lye potion euphemistically called "bleaching creme," desperate to get light enough to escape the effect of racism. I remember my grandmother burning my scalp with a hot "straightening comb," so my hair's natural kinkiness would not offend white classmates. I looked down at my brown skin, almost invisible in the darkness as I drove, and shuddered.

I parked the car in front of the apartment building where I live. Large chunks of peeling paint hang from the walls to expose aging plaster underneath. Graffiti created by children with no other canvas for their thoughts fills the entryway walls. Steel bars on doors and windows protect my apartment from the intrusions of burglars and desperate junkies. As I open the door, I see the walls, a nondescript grey color from layers of grease, smoke and dust. The worn furniture and the stained carpet feed my growing depression.

I have lived in this apartment for ten years. I no longer go confidently apartment-hunting, with my employment and credit histories in hand like the reins to a high-spirited horse. I have come home from too many such expeditions discouraged and disappointed, trapped in this "ghetto" against my

will. I even filed a discrimination complaint once, only to
have the owner sneer at me as he paid his fine, certain that he
would still rent to a white tenant. The apartment I live in,
despite its limitations, saves me from the humiliation and
degradation of apartment-hunting anywhere in Los Angeles
County, from Glendale to Malibu.

I remembered Angela Davis exhorting us to "take it to
the streets!" I needed an action or solution to make me feel
powerful again. The faceless landlord in Glendale had returned me to the fear and impotence I felt in 1956 when
owners could refuse openly to rent to Blacks. I got out of my
car, walked over to the peeling paint, and grabbed a large
chunk. I took it in the apartment and wrote across it with a
large black marker: "REMEMBER!" It sits on the desk
where I write.

Requiescat in Pacem

She was a refugee
forced to emigrate
from the war zone of my body

tanks rolled through
the silent peace shattered
machine gun bursts of pain
rained on her spirit
his blows a staccato bludgeon
on my belly
crushing her mind
killing her spirit

trapped naked
in the warm pool of my womb
defenseless against the violence
raging outside
her amniotic shield ruptured
no safe shelter even there

she was a refugee
forced to emigrate
from the war zone of my body

brought into the world
with eyes glazed and frightened
reflecting torture endured
muscles twitching and convulsing
head jerking at the slightest sound
young heart barely pumping
prematurely aged by her ordeal
wounds inside and out

she was a refugee
fleeing pain and confusion
all the unanswered questions

her father/the soldier
whose blows drove her
from her home/from herself
from his violence
relentlessly pursued
his misogynistic guest
recriminations like bullets
tearing through her consciousness
fueled by alcohol

armed with twin missiles of racism and sexism

he never looked back
never saw the gouged earth
rotted crops
gutted homes
wasted child
until she was gone

our first child
nestled in my fecund womb
terrified by armored carriers
the rhythm of marching feet
the anguished screams of this war
forced to run from mortal shells
no place to grow or flourish
in the barren devastation of our war

no medics, no Red Cross
her young heart bled
her spirit wailed

she was a casualty of our war
her death a temporary armistice
the only peace she could find
in the blood-soaked trenches
where the war continues

Judith McDaniel

The Descent

She lived in a time when stability
not change   was the key to safety
a time that said dismantling the missiles
and warheads was   destabilizing
Balance   she heard them say   requires stasis
but she saw smoke hovering on the horizon
of every city she drove toward and held
in her memory   the hawk balanced
on a trembling wing   and she knew
the old tree grown rigid against the wind
was the tree that fell.
                              And yet for years
her worst nightmare found her in an unknown
future   alone without a landscape. Nothing
in that nightmare future was familiar—
nostalgia was connected to a known and vanished
past.   She'd wake   touch the woman
sleeping familiarly close   and sleep again
sure the dream was just a fluke
surely   surely   she knew what her future
held   knew that potential landscape
as surely as she knew the arm she touched.

The rooms grew darker imperceptibly
the rooms in which she lived her life
and tried to build a present filled
with light. Looking back she could find
no single moment   no single room
or voice or face to mark the turning

when the circle became a spiral
when the way led only down.

> *I always wanted what I*
> *was not supposed to want.*
> *I don't remember the child*
> *of four or five who told*
> *the reporter she wanted*
> *to be a boy named Tommy*
> *and own a pet pig   but*
> *last year my grandmother*
> *gave me the clipping*
> *out of the family bible*
> *and there I was   wide-eyed*
> *and smiling. Why not Tommy?*
> *My script read different:*
> *college   marry mommy.*
> *I tried to take the cues*
> *that came my way*
> *but that other me held back*
> *clamped down tight*
> *I waited.*

She drank when she was tired for the strength
to see her through, she drank when she was angry
for the strength to hold it back, she drank
when she felt strongly so the feeling wouldn't
show, she drank when she felt nothing
to bring the feeling back. She
drank when she was the only one, the different
one, the one who had to make the difference
who had to lead the way, who showed where
to begin. She drank when being different
made others feel afraid, left her standing
all alone.

Nice. That was the thing
in our family, that I should
be nice—no matter what else,
the neighbors should know
how nice I was. Be nice,
what a nice girl, how cute.
Tommy, you say?
So when I stood up
in front of all those people
who wanted me to do something
or be someone, I wanted them
to like me and think I was nice
even when I was telling them that
who I was went against everything
they ever believed in or even
when I was telling them to fight,
to believe in themselves
and fight for what they needed,
still I thought they should think
I was nice. Once I told a friend
I thought people should like me
more, since I was basically
nice. Nice? she asked. Nice?
Don't sell yourself short.
You're not nice.

Peace seemed worth having, personal
peace, the place she could go deep
inside herself and not have to listen
to the voices. Sometimes weeding
the garden, writing in a journal, hearing
different music and the call of each bird,
then she felt at peace. But more often
she would hear the voice and remember
her script and so she would answer

and go and be or do whatever
was required.
                    And when she had to shut
them out she drank and when she had to go
out to meet them she drank and when
she drank she thought it was they who
would not let her in
                        So that the rooms
grew darker and the air she breathed seemed
to have all been breathed before.

> *I shook all day of the night*
> *I went to talk about how maybe*
> *I was ready to think about*
> *not drinking. I'd been alone*
> *for two weeks, told myself I didn't*
> *have a problem. Others made it up.*
> *And if no one was there to see*
> *I'd find my natural level. I did.*
> *And couldn't breathe at all when*
> *I woke up. I was scared.*
> *Scared. I didn't know why*
> *but I was shaking inside and it*
> *worked its way out to my hands*
> *and my voice when I spoke. All day*
> *I said, hey, it's nothing to be*
> *afraid of, and I was afraid.*
> *I'd thought that death was the end*
> *of changing, but this change*
> *felt like death.*

Later she would put the lies in here too
but she hadn't gotten that far then—
couldn't see how she'd found the peace
by lying. She used the lies to shut

them all out, to create a false and private
place, and finally the lies
came between her and the woman sleeping
close, and when she'd reach to touch
her arm, she wasn't sure
who she would find there.

We each come differently to that place
where there is nothing left. We reach out
to touch firm ground and find
we've already gone down further even
than that and there is no room to turn,
to shift, no room to move at all
or breathe. The earth sat on her chest
like yesterday's promises.

> *I felt like an animal*
> *gnawing my own leg*
> *to get out of the trap*
> *and the blood tasted*
> *like metal.*

She breathed quietly the mute untested
air of the world in which she woke,
longed for the welcoming songs
without knowing what she longed for,
because she feared this change
like death and she came—a different
kind of creature—back into this
world where yesterday today and tomorrow
were supposed to be the same, a world
in which the old ways were the good ways,
and yet for her the old ways led
only to that place where there was nothing
left and when she came to that place

she knew it now for what it was
and turning she began the journey out.

Coming Back
for Audre Lorde

Out of these winter depths
a voice summons me:
the only pain that is unbearable
is wasted pain   always there is
something to be learned. I flinch
step back from this voice
that would take me
to the hard places.

I tell you now
I am afraid.

Ice was on the road   ice
was building in the stream
and drooping from the boughs
of every tree as the structure
of my familiar world
seemed to stretch
and then collapse.

Ice bends the white birch into a bow
under its weight   the tree
broken   glittering   in the deceptive
beauty of winter   will not grow
straight up after the thaw.

I became that Minnesota woman

trapped in a nightmare of failure
of risks not visible   when unprotected
and alone at sixty below zero
like her I walked   slowing
toward a destination I could never reach.
The wind shrilled under my short coat
and I slowed   as I walked
each foot a separate effort
the only sound within.

On that ice bound road I watched
my stiffening body   how my shoulders
ceased to sway as outside
the earth accelerated   stars kaleidoscoped
seemed to move so fast each path merged
ribbons of light to my slowing eye
past and future slide on the iced wind
as I moved within   as I seemed
to be not here to those outside.

I could have let go
felt the sharpness grow numb
released the pain   walked away
from what I once knew
walked that road swept clean
by wind and snow as though
no one had been here before
as though a voice were not echoing
the only pain that is unbearable
is wasted pain.

if there were silence
if the only voice was the wind's voice
if I pulled all sensation back within

I could begin
the letting go.

But today I choose the journey back
acknowledge the damage   anticipate
the painful thaw   not restitution
a recovery more moderate   more slow.
They found her body cordwood stiff
no pulse or breath discernible
and brought her back each step reversed:

the shard of ice melts from behind our eyes
and we must see again and move again
and know again
what we would not choose to know.

WE PULL OFF THE ROAD JUST PAST AMARILLO

We pull off the road just past Amarillo
at anywhere Texas a red dirt road
divides the horizon   hiccups over _
a railroad crossing and goes on forever.

My jogging shoes follow the lacechain track
of birds—ground nesters I guess—
scanning the fields there is no tree
anywhere and I can see tomorrow.

I run away from the car toward the tracks.
New York plates. Two women running.
I imagine a cop standing by the car

when we return—a fantasy for sure—
out here I couldn't run far enough
to lose sight of the car.

You girls scared? No. I am not running
because I am scared. The sky out here
is so wide I could fall up into it
if I were to lift both feet off the ground
but this does not scare me. And authority
does not scare me today. Though I have never
been anywhere I could tell the good guys
from the bad.

At night we bed down close to the earth
and she pulls me back from the sky
and sometimes it is this that scares me
being this close to the earth.

Louise Moore

History

I know woman's more correct,
but yeah, I still call women I know
girl.
I do it to remember.

Sure I come from the woman's movement,
but I also come from
Knoxville, Tennessee
1970's gay bars.

Some of the men there
still called each other
Mary and Miz Thing.

And, some of the women
drank too much, cut their hair
like men, and beat up on their lovers.

But, in the good times
When some woman came in through the door
One of the women would push a chair out
from a table with her foot, and call across the room.
"Hey girl, come on over here!"

Mrs. McKinnis Thinks It's Spring

Mrs. McKinnis was always the first one every
year to put away her winter coat. No matter how grey and
cold it still was in the city, when the first of March came
around Mrs. McKinnis insisted it was spring.

She would start right away wearing those little spring
dresses and sometimes even sandals. Even when she had
goose bumps on her arms--when you asked if she was cold,
she always replied no.

Finally, last year, Mrs. McKinnis was badly ill. She was even
admitted to the hospital. She had caught a bad case of pneu-
monia. It was touch and go for some time, but she came out
of it okay, though very weak. Her doctor and all her friends
scolded Mrs. McKinnis long and hard.

At last Mrs. McKinnis had to admit that it wasn't spring.
Now she checks her indoor-outdoor thermometer before she
goes out. She wears a coat when it's cold out.

Mrs. McKinnis had to face the facts. Near spring now, she
begins to grow hyacinths in the windows of her living room.

Mrs. McKinnis In Her Garden

In early spring, Mrs. McKinnis went to the nursery to buy a
bush for her yard. Over on the side of the nursery leaning
against the chain link fence, she saw what she thought was a
bush. She liked it, and since she was in a hurry she bought it
without any questions.

When Mrs. McKinnis got home she rushed to the shed, got out her shovel, and planted her purchase. She watered it faithfully. It began to grow.

One day as Mrs. McKinnis was looking out her window, she was perplexed to notice that the bush had grown almost as tall as the garage roof. It wasn't very pretty either--more like a scrub, and it still hadn't flowered. She took a leaf back to the nursery, and they told her that what she had thought was a bush was a lilac tree.

Mrs. McKinnis had wanted a bush. She really did not want a tree. A tree would take over the yard. Leaves would get everywhere. It wouldn't flower for at least another year. Mrs. McKinnis went out and pruned the tree down to bush proportions. The tree kept growing. She stopped watering the tree.

It still grew. She went out and pruned again. And again and again. Two months later, Mrs. McKinnis looked out and there the tree was, back up to the garage roof. She went outside with a glass of lemonade, drank lemonade and stared at the tree. Mrs. McKinnis went a little crazy. She grabbed the axe from the woodpile and chopped at the tree until only a stub was left. Breathing a sigh of relief, Mrs. McKinnis went inside.

It was a long cold winter. The storm shutters stayed on the windows till late in the spring. It was the middle of May before Mrs. McKinnis had time for the garden.

As she came around the corner from the shed with her tools she looked over by the wall. There stood the lilac full of purple blossoms, towering over the garage roof. It was still a tree. Mrs. McKinnis dropped her tools and sat down on the ground, laughing.

Brenda Weathers
Communion

ONE AFTER ANOTHER, yellowed leaves drifted past the window pane. Beyond the near, bare branches lay the dark waters of the Sound. Mountain peaks on the far side of the water loomed in dark silhouette against the sky.

Marjorie Mason turned her gaze slowly from the view outside her bedroom window toward her legs, thin ridges angling across the bed and barely disturbing the light blanket Ceil had placed over her as the day began to cool.

Light slanted through the window in a yellow rectangle, blanketing Marjorie and the bed where she lay. It felt good, that covering of light, comforting to a body grown frail, a body evaporating life as surely as the sun evaporated water from an August creekbed.

In the earlier days of her illness, she had used the image of the sun's brilliance, seeing it fill her body and scrub clean the places where disease intruded. And even now, she welcomed the light's warmth spreading over her in a balm more gentle than any offered by the array of bottles at her bedside.

Marjorie looked again to the window. Now that most of the leaves had fallen, she could see the narrow path leading to the rocks along the water's edge. For twenty years she had walked that path, and for twenty years things had ever changed and remained the same.

Sometimes, as now, the trees leaves were gold, sometimes green. The water was emerald or it was blue. Marjorie's hair turned from dark brown to silver. But, of whatever color, the sea was always there, and the trees, and Marjorie with her striding gait and her mission. She had walked that path in every climate and season, but on evenings in early summer, she had walked it with a more purposeful stride.

The first summer she and Ceil had lived at the house at the

water's edge, Marjorie had excused herself one evening after supper to take a solitary walk along the beach. The sun hung like an orange ball between peaks of blue on that long-ago evening. Ripples on the water's surface glittered tinsel-like pink.

For a long while, Marjorie had stared out across the water, arms clasped around her drawn up knees, her back propped against a rock. She breathed deeply of the pungent ocean and allowed her gaze to wander without expectation between fingers of pastel clouds and the darkening horizon.

Suddenly she stopped her gaze. Several large shapes moved slowly through the water in the middle distance. They seemed to be heading toward the spot where she sat, and she watched intently for several seconds, then gasped as a whale soared from the surface, splaying water in all directions, then dove again, its fins like dark wings against the sky.

Marjorie clung to the rock and did not move. Carried by her imagination or perhaps by some trick of the wind, she fancied she heard the otherworldly singing of the whales. The music, for music she knew the sounds to be, held her transfixed and longing, aching, to cross between her world and theirs. She yearned for the meanings held in the strange and yet not unfamiliar sounds, and to know of the intimacies shared out there in the deep, cold water.

How terribly lonely, she thought, that we sing but only for our own, that we strive yet can never really breech the separations of creation, one from the other.

Marjorie did not leave the rock until the sun was well down and early evening chill brought gooseflesh to her brown arms. But she returned to the rock the next evening and every summer evening after that.

For twenty years and more, when the whales came to their summer place, Marjorie came to the shore to greet them. On each occasion, she brought with her a battered music stand and her oboe. Balancing her cargo, she stepped out onto the rock and set the stand facing the water, using clothespins to secure the many pages of quarter notes, half notes and glissandos. She took her oboe from its case, and with it her longing, and began to play.

She never knew whether the whales heard her music, the Bach she played, or the Mozart, or, sometimes, the music she made up for herself. But she played as if they did. She played with her breath and her fingers and her heart, wanting to believe they heard and, like her, were mystified and curious and filled with longing.

How quickly it all changes, Marjorie thought, still looking through her window down at the path. How like juggler's pins everything really is; how very like life the colorful balancing act. In one instant, all is in order, carefully thrown patterns moving in time and space, existing yet changing in the same moment--never touching, yet incomplete without those gone before and those to follow.

Then, in less than a breath, one pin falls. The delicate circle breaks. The pins roll away, tumbling across the floor--out of order--out of control, breaking the pattern, no matter how bright or inventive.

Before such a moment, she had been Marjorie Mason, poet. Marjorie who loved to garden and called herself friend to life. She had been Marjorie who loved and lived with Ceil in their house of glass and sunlight at the water's edge. Then, in the next moment, she became someone in possession of unwelcome facts, a woman with appointments to keep and with a looming date to bear in mind. In the tiresome sameness of clinics and hospitals, she came to be known as a diagnosis rather than by a verse she especially liked or for the ruby red gladiolas in her garden.

Marjorie stirred slightly and winced. Ceil would be up soon, bringing a mug of broth Marjorie would only pretend to sip. It would make Ceil feel better though, the pretense of sipping food, taking nourishment from rounded blue mugs

Ceil had fashioned in their pottery shed.

It would be hardest on Ceil, of course. Ceil with her determination and her regime of soups and grains, concoctions lovingly offered from the whirring blender. These are my weapons, her eyes said, these and my love. Ceil would be the hardest. Hard to leave her mourning death and mourning, too, perhaps, the failure of her soups and her love.

The pool of light receded from the bed as the sun lowered to the horizon. Marjorie shifted her gaze to the bedside table and the jumble of bottles, wadded tissues and blue basins. She opened a drawer and carefully removed a slim brown vial, one she opened only to fill. She jiggled the vial and looked intently at her hoard of red capsules. There were enough now--had been for some time. More than enough, in fact, waiting only for the right moment.

Each day now, as Ceil sat with Marjorie, her hands resting lightly over Marjorie's thin one, careful of the yellow bruises from all those needles, she asked with her eyes, "Today?" and Marjorie answered with hers, "No. Not yet."

When they first learned Marjorie was ill, they returned from the clinic with the terrible words thundering in their ears. Marjorie had sat at the kitchen table holding a bottle of medicine, dispensed in place of hope. She held the vial between thumb and forefinger, peering quizzically at it and slowly shaking her head. "You know," she had said, "I've not taken so much as a whole bottle of aspirin in my entire life." Ceil, watching Marjorie watch the bottle, had been aware that the geranium in the window box needed a good watering. If only she could turn things backward--wake up all over again this morning and just not keep that appointment at the clinic. If she could somehow do that, she could get up and go water that geranium, perhaps fix a little lunch. Marjorie could go off to her studio, a cramped room overflowing with books and papers in poetical disorder. She could bury herself there--bury herself! So ordinary a phrase.

Ordinary until today, when, even unspoken, it hung like brass in the air between them.

Ceil had watched helplessly as a tear slid from Marjorie's eye to the burnished oak table. The two women were immediately clutching one another, each showering the other with hugs and caresses, gesures of reassurance and desperation.

"You know," Marjorie had said, straightening, then running a hand through her cropped hair. "It's not the dying I mind so much, it's the being sick I'll hate." She jammed her hands into her jacket pocket and looked past the geranium in the window box to the sunlit afternoon. "I dread having to stop doing what I enjoy, like my walks along the beach, my concerts for the whales. But, the worst of it is," she said, looking directly at Ceil, "the worst of it is--I don't want to become a burden." Ceil tried to shush her, but Marjorie went on anyway. "I've thought about this before, what would I do if ever something like this happened. I can't bear the thought of becoming a burden--of becoming helpless. I won't allow it. I won't subject either of us to so cruel a parting." Marjorie had locked her gaze on Ceil, daring that she not be misunderstood.

Marjorie turned slowly, painfully, on the pillow. That conversation seemed so long ago now, yet it had only taken place last spring. Now here it was fall again. So soon, it seemed, the night air had grown chilly, the leaves gone from green to bright red.

Ceil's footsteps sounded on the stairs. Marjorie heard the tinkle of silverware on a tray. Ceil appeared in the doorway and stood there a moment before entering. "Are you in pain?" she whispered as she moved toward the bed. "Yes," Marjorie answered, barely able to mouth the sound. She spoke so seldom anymore, and when she did, her voice sounded foreign to her, as if coming from someone smaller than she and further away. When awake, she spoke to the ever-present Ceil, but with increasing difficulty. But she was awake so seldom now. Time was impossible to measure.

Ceil set the tray on the table and handed a mug of broth across to Marjorie. Marjorie stopped her with a weak clasp of her wrist. "I don't think I'll be having any soup today," she managed. "Set the cup down."

Ceil bent closer, looking at Marjorie and seeing, instead of the shriveled and fragile form on the bed, a more robust Marjorie, remembering eyes that once shone aquamarine in morning's first light. She held her breath and waited, gently stroking Marjorie's arm, waiting and knowing and not wanting to know at all.

It would be Marjorie's decision, of course. On that they had agreed. Marjorie and Marjorie alone would decide when the day had come. She would know when to open the vial of capsules, this time not to add but to remove it.

There had come a point when they knew, both of them, that Marjorie was going to die. The soup and the love, the prayers and the hope had done a mightly battle but, even so, Marjorie was slipping away. And, somewhere near this stark certainty, Marjorie began to take on a cast of death. Steadily she diminished. Everything about her seemed to pale and grow smaller: her frame, her eyes, the reach of her mind while awake and, finally, the amount of time she was conscious of the world around her. Everything grew smaller but the pain.

At first, Ceil had resisted the idea of hoarding pills, could not bring herself to think of sitting at Marjorie's side while she filled her mouth with death. But Marjorie, growing steadily weaker, had kept talking of such a day. In time, she came to speak of it, not with timidity, fear or resentment, but with gentleness and longing, such a longing she had once felt while playing Bach and Mozart for the whales.

Ceil still held Marjorie's hand. For an uncounted length of time, the silence in the upstairs bedroom was disturbed only by the rasp of Marjorie's breathing and the tick of a clock.

"Today," Marjorie rasped and fell into a sleep.

Sometime later, as shadows lenghtened across the floor, Marjorie stirred.   Ceil pressed a   moistened towel to Marjorie's lips.   "There's something I'd like," Marjorie whispered and held Ceil's cool hand to her cheek. "I've been trying to see out of the window--down the path to the beach." Marjorie paused to gather strength, then went on. "But, I'm so weak now--and the light is fading."

"Of course," Ceil said quickly. "I'll prop you up so you can have a better view."

"No. Not that. I want to go down there."

"But, it's evening," Ceil said. "It'll be getting chilly soon. Of course, I'll take you there. But you know the whales are gone. It's much too late in the year for them. I haven't seen one in weeks."

"Even so," Marjorie gasped, coughing. "Even so, it's the place I've always loved best. I want to go there--be there when I...."

Ceil nodded and swooped the vial of pills into her shirt pocket. "Let me get a blanket to throw over you."

"Yes, and that cider we put up last Halloween--and the crystal goblets."

Marjorie was light in Ceil's arms. Her eyes were closed against the pain of the slightest jostle, yet she knew with all her senses every detail of the path they travelled. There were the lilac bushes and just beyond them the place where the path turned from gravel to sand as it made the last turn for the shore.

There was the sound of waves lapping the beach and wind rustling the trees. Marjorie drank deeply of these smells and sounds. Her favorite world.

Suddenly, Ceil cried out. "Look, Marjorie. Look to the horizon!"

Slowly, Marjorie opened her eyes, already knowing what

Ceil had seen there.

Several large grey whales dotted the horizon, swimming and diving toward the shore and Marjorie, the night air swelling with their familiar singing. The whales!

Pauline Moore

GOOD FRIENDS

Chorus Good friends, play-ing to-geth-er, stay-ing to-geth-er good

friends   Tak-ing the time to op-en your mind to good

friends.   Al- ways learn- ing some-thing sec-

- ret that is bur- ied in the soul, Can

you re- veal it as we strive to make it whole

Don't con-ceal   it there is noth-ing now to hide

it's safe to come out side.

arms are ope- n wide ope n ope n to you.

Second verse:

winds are blowing, seasons changing and nothing stays the same
Re-arranging but no one is to blame
wheels are turning but we're caught inside the flame
Rising, falling, rising and falling, again, and again and again
and again and again.

Biographies of Contributors

Paula Gunn Allen: Laguna Pueblo-Sioux-Scottish-American and Lebanese American. Currently a professor at UC Berkeley, she teaches classes in Ethnic Studies/Native American Studies . She has received two post-doctoral fellowships and an NEA writer's grant. Her prose and poetry have appeared widely in anthologies, journals and scholarly publications, in addition to her books. She lives in the Bay Area with her son.

Judye A.Best (cover artist): Born on income tax day in Heber Springs, Arkansas, she grew up in a strong Pentecostal religious family. Best has changed her religion to Nichiren Shoshu of American Buddhism. To earn her living she manages a retail store that sells art posters. Her ambitions in life are to be happy and healthy one day at a time. She is a member of Alcoholic Anonymous.

Ashley Black: She grew up in Chicago, spent her twenties in Washington, DC., married, and along with her husband became a lieutenant in the Marine Corps. Leaving both her husband and the service, she took up residence in San Francisco and wrote a teleplay called *Cloistered.* She entered UCLA's film school and there wrote a number of feature-length scripts. She works as an advertising copywriter.

SDiane Bogus: Publisher of W.I.M. Publications, as well as a poet and professor, she has published her work and others under her own imprint and in other publications, such as *Sackbut Review, Black American Literature Forum* and *Sinister Wisdom..* She recently completed her doctoral work on Ann Shockley and Emily Dickinson.

Jeri Castronova: Writing poetry since childhood, she considers it "sacred therapy." She has published a book of poetry, *Shadow of the Goddess*. She is Los Angeles-based, has a doctorate in Clinical Psychology and leads workshops in rituals of transformation, building creativity, past life therapy, and healing the inner child. She teaches at the Healing Light Center and has a private practice.

Jacqueline de Angelis: Born and raised in Youngstown, Ohio, she has lived in Los Angeles for 18 years. She has been published in literary magazines and has a book out, *Main Gate* (Paradise Press). Along with Aleida Rodriguez, she was co-founder of *rara avis* magazine and Books of a Feather Press. She received a writer-in-residence fellowship from Dorland Mountain Colony in 1984.

Marie Jose Delgado: Born in El Puerto de Santa Maria, Spain, she grew up in a large extended family. At 13 her mother accused her of being a lesbian when she found a love poem. At 20 she left Spain to follow her lover to America and worked at a shelter for battered women in Los Angeles and is currently finishing a masters degree in Spanish Literature. She lives in Tucson, Arizona.

Ayofemi Stowe Folayan: She has been synthesizing her creative energies and political beliefs for more than twenty years. She has performed as an actress and musician with the National Black Theatre in New York City. In addition to the short stories in this collection, she is one of the authors of *Pursuit of Happiness*. She also a co-author with Podolsky of a performance piece that explores the realities of racism, anti-semitism, homophobia and classism.

Nancy Tyler Glenn: Los Angeles native Glenn operates her own lesbian bookstore, Clicking Stones, which is relocating to Sante Fe, New Mexico. The store is named after her book, *Clicking Stones,* to be released in the spring of 1989 by Naiad press. When Nancy isn't writing or selling books, she's teaching improvisational theatre, assisting in an art performance project, playing with her cat ZahZee or at the race track.

Judy Grahn: She has been a familiar name in the Gay movement. For over twenty years she's been an activist, a poet and a publisher. She had her work in many publications, as well as having published several books. In addition she teaches Gay and Lesbian studies in San Francisco. Her book, *Another Mother Tongue*, won the 1985 Gay Book Award of the American Library Association.

Eloise Klein Healy: Her poems have appeared in numerous literary magazines as well as her books. She's taught at Immaculate Heart College, The Wright Institute and elsewhere. She has taught and served on the Board of Directors of the Woman's Building. Recipient of a residency at Dorland Mountain Colony, a fellowship to the MacDowell Colony and a Vesta Award from the Woman's Building, she has been recognized for her contibution to women and the arts in Southern California.

Chaney Holland: Author and activist Chaney Holland is the associate producer of a new educational video designed to foster positive images of lesbians, produced by Connexxus. Currently, she is developing a series of poems about virginal images in the psyche. Her work has appeared in various literary magazines. She teaches writing in Tucson, Arizona.

Bia Lowe: She has been published in anthologies and literary magazines and is the co-author, with performer Leslie Belt, of the comedy, *All About Betty* , which was produced at LA's Theatre of Arts, summer 1988. Currently she is working on a series of essays concerning urban wildlife. When not writing, she is a drummer, a designer and a homemaker.

Judith McDaniel: Poet and fiction writer, she lives in Albany, New York. Her most recent book, *Sanctuary: A Journey,* contains poems and essays about her experience in Central America as well as her acquaintance with the Central American refugees in the U.S.

M'Lissa Mayo: Her roots in the arts reach back more than 20 years. Poet, actress, multi-media performer, Mayo's performances include *Mother Earth and Father Time are Getting Divorced I & II.* Her print work has been published in several anthologies and group works including *Yippie Yi Yo Cahier* . She expects to complete her first book in Spring of 1989. Meanwhile, M'Lissa resides in peace in West Hollywood.

karen marie christa minns: She has published in literary magazines throughout the world, among them are *Sinister Wisdom, On Our Backs* and Britain's *Maniacs' Diary.* Her work has also been widely published in anthologies such as *Voices in the Night* and *The Wings, The Vines: four women poets.* Her current novel, a lesbian vampire love story, *Virago*, will be published by Naiad in 1989.

Louise Moore: An escapee from the South, she has lived in Los Angeles for nine years. Since publication of her book of poems, *Heartland,* in 1986, she has turned to storytelling. Her tales focus on the importance of the small happenings of the everyday.

Pauline Moore: She is a professional musician, teacher, performer, minstrel. Singer/songwriter, healer and composer, she resides in Sierra Madre, California. She came from Bath, England to pursue her interest in healing arts. She also found in California a liberated women's community which enticed her to stay. Her main interest is healing through music by chanting. Cassettes of her music are commercially available.

Eileen Pagan: Several years ago, Pagan left her native Puerto Rico for New York City. This poet/memoirist now makes her home in Los Angeles.

Marlene Pearson: Her poems have appeared in literary magazines such as Calyx. She won the Rachel Sherwood Poetry Prize and an Academy of American Poets Award. She is teaching and pursuing a graduate degree from California State University, Northridge.

Robin Podolsky: She has stealthily propagated her poetry and prose, she says, throughout Los Angeles through such cultural outposts as the *L.A. Weekly*, the Woman's Building, the Lhasa Club, Gorky's Cafe, Anti-Club and *The Lesbian News*. Her first play, *Pursuit of Happiness*, co-written with four others premiered at Celebration Theater in 1986.

Lynette Prucha: By day a film executive in the entertainment industry, by night a novelist. She has a master's in Comparative Literature from the University of Southern California. She looks forward to working on a second novel entitled, *World Without Men, Amen*.

Gloria Ramos: She was born in New York City into a Puerto Rican environment. She left New York, fell in love with Los Angeles and now lives in Santa Monica. She loves writing but has not submitted any work previously. She says that now, "Maybe I will send out some others that are hiding in my bottom drawer." She is currently working on an expanded version of *Rush Hour Bunny*.

Carol Schmidt: She has been a newspaper reporter, magazine editor, public relations director, college instructor. In 1984 she received the Gay and Lesbian Press Association's Outstanding Lesbian Journalist award. Her life partner, Norma Hair, and she own a tax consultant business, Words & Numbers, and spend summers/ falls renovating their 1871 church home in rural Michigan. Mostly, she writes novels.

Sharon Stricker: An L.A. based poet/writer, her work has appeared in *Heresies, Dreamworks, The Venice Beachhead, Cafe Solo, The L.A. Catalyst, The Prison Writing Review*. For five years she was editor, producer and publisher of *Poppy*, the Women's Creative Writing Journal, while a California Arts Council Resident Artist. She co-founded and directed Bright Fires Creative Writing Program at California Rehabilitation Center, medium security prison for men and women. Her work at CRC was recently featured on "Voices from the Pen," a half-hour video documentary made by KCET-TV in 1987.

Brenda Weathers: Founder and first director of the Alcoholism Center for Women in Los Angeles, she now lives on Vashon Island in Puget Sound, a ferry ride from Seattle. She and her lover live with several animals and run a Mom and Mom frozen yogurt/pizza stand called Brief Encounters. In 1986 Naiad published her lesbian ghost story called, *The House at Pelham Falls*.

Carolyn Weathers: Writer, librarian and activist, she is the author of *Crazy, Leaving Texas, Shitkickers & Other Texas Stories,* and her work appeared in the anthology, *My*

Story's On: Ordinary Women/ Extraordinary Lives (Common Differences Press). Her play, *Mouse Soup,* was produced at Los Angeles' Celebration Theatre fall 1987. She is part of the LA Committee to Free Sharon Kowalski. She lives and overworks with artist/publisher/information specialist Jenny Wrenn, in Los Angeles.

Jess Wells: A San Franciscan, she is the author of several books, including her most recent *A Herstory of Prostitution in Western Europe.* Her work has appeared in many literary magazines and on the stage of the Michigan Womyn's Music Festival. Driven by the desire to be self-employed in fiction, she self-publishes her work under the name of Library B Books.

Terry Wolverton: She leads the multiple lives of writer, arts administrator, writing instructor, and management consultant. Her poetry, fiction, dramatic scripts, theory, features and art criticism have been published internationally. Her work has appeared in the following anthologies: *Southern California Women Writers and Artists* (Books of a Feather), *Learning Our Way* (Crossing Press), *Between Ourselves: Letters Between Mothers and Daughters* (Houghton Mifflin) and *Voices in the Night* (Cleis Press).

Ruchele ZeOeh: Retired from social work, she began to write poetry six years ago. Her work has appeared in *Poetry/ LA, Sinister Wisdom, Project Rainbow.* She has read her poetry throughout Los Angeles. For the past three years, she has worked on a one act, all womyn play, *T.O.P. Togetherness.*